According to my earnest expectation and my hope,
that in nothing I shall be ashamed,
but that with all boldness, as always,
so now also Christ shall be magnified in my body,
whether it be by life, or by death.
For to me to live is Christ, and to die is gain.
Phil. 1:20-21

But we all, with open face
beholding as in a glass the glory of the Lord,
are changed into the same image from glory to glory,
even as by the Spirit of the Lord.
2 Cor. 3:18

CHRIST
MAGNIFIED

GLORIFYING JESUS BY YOUR LIFE

JAMES S. HOLLANDSWORTH

NOLLYPUBLISHING

The Bible version used in this publication
is the King James Version.

ISBN-10: 0-9963596-2-1

ISBN-13: 978-0-9963596-2-7

Printed in the United States of America

Dedication

To my seven children:
Katie, Josh, Phil, Rachel, Anna, Beth & Sarah
May you glorify Jesus throughout your lives.

I have no greater joy than to hear
that my children walk in truth.
3 John 4

and …

To my dear Aussie friends from Melbourne:
Pastor Ernest & Liz Veszely
Benjy, Ande, Antoinette, Carol, and Fionna
Our meeting in Israel was Providential.
Your conference theme inspired me
to write this book.
God bless you!

Acknowledgements

I am truly grateful to my dear friends
who willingly reviewed this book before publication
and gave valuable input, both grammatical and theological.
Thank you for your wisdom and insight.
I am honored to have your friendship.

Matthew Barfield
Keith Call
Marty Cauley
Ernest Childs
Scott Crawford
Tracy Daniels
Alan Robinson
Lewis & Charlotte Schoettle
Todd Tjepkema

Contents

Preface

Magnifiers and Reflectors

My Confession

I remember well the day in my early childhood when I stumbled across the basic scientific principles of magnification and reflection. It was the combination of the two that got me into trouble one lovely sunny morning. It started with the innocent activity of "frying" ants on the sidewalk with the magnifying glass recently given to me by my grandmother. I was entertained by watching the smoke that resulted when the magnified sun became focused on the little critters on the sidewalk. But boredom quickly set in.

Remembering the magnification mirror on my mother's dresser, I covertly borrowed it and returned outdoors to apply the principle of magnification in new and grander ways. Noticing the parochial school across the street in my Chicago neighborhood, I could see through the row of large windows the backs of the heads of the school children as they sat facing their teacher, a nun from the Catholic diocese. She was looking in my direction. I wondered, out of curiosity, what would happen if magnification and reflection were to be used together. So I squatted under my neighbor's front porch, out of sight, and used the magnification mirror to reflect the sun's light into the classroom across the street. The effect was far greater than imagined. The blast of light shone brightly into the nun's eyes like a heavenly vision, distracting all the students, who turned around to discover the source of light. I quickly ducked back under the porch, carefully peering out to see the chaos I had caused as a result of my "science" experiment.

Once order had been restored to the classroom, I repeated the experiment three or four times, either out of a desire to test my hypothesis or out of sheer enjoyment; I can't remember which. Within minutes, the teacher realized the reflection was not coincidental but intentional, and soon I found myself being chased through the neighborhood by two nuns wielding thick rulers as weapons of punishment. Scared to death, being just a young child, I ran through an alley and found a basement stairwell as a place of hiding. I remained there for quite some time — perhaps an hour or more — waiting for the vigilante nuns to give up their search for the child criminal. Thankfully, they never found me. Needless to say, early on I learned that magnification and reflection work quite well together. Indeed, when combined, they get the point across emphatically.

On a More Spiritual Note

Unfortunately, it was not until my adult years when I learned the powerful effects of magnifying Christ (Phil. 1:20) and reflecting His image (2 Cor. 3:18), through my life, in this present world. It is the duty of every child of God, and if applied faithfully, culminates in Christ being glorified and the saint rewarded. Is that not our ultimate objective for living?

> Whether therefore ye eat, or drink, or whatsoever ye do, do all to the glory of God. 1 Cor. 10:31

I memorized this verse as a child and was reminded regularly through the years by parents, pastors, and teachers of my responsibility to glorify God. We often sang the hymn, "To God Be the Glory," in our church, so the concept was never far from my mind. I took this truth for granted and never questioned it, since it is plainly Scriptural. Nevertheless, it became stale to me over time, developing more into a lifeless theological plank in my doctrinal statement rather than a lively purpose statement evidenced in my everyday thinking and behavior. In other words, I could give a quick, concise, catechismal answer to the question, "What is your ultimate purpose in life?" but it wasn't really my purpose in practice. Though I wasn't living like an unbeliever, I am ashamed to say that my passion was not focused on glorifying the Lord. Self was in the way. I would never have admitted it at the time, but now in hindsight I can see more plainly.

I am truly thankful for God's mercy and patience. He never gave up on me, and He kept after me. The Hound of Heaven (and I use the term reverently) stayed on my trail. He taught me *how* to glorify God. I have learned the secret of cooperating with Christ who lives within me, appropriating His grace, in order that I might magnify and reflect Him by my life. Not that I am always victorious, but at least I now understand not only *what* is to be done but also *how* to do it. I experience patterns of victory more than patterns of defeat. For that, I am most grateful to my Lord.

A Multi-Faceted Diamond

The purpose of this book is to demonstrate from the Scriptures how we, as children of God, can magnify Christ and reflect Him by our lives. Along the way we will also discover the glorious benefits for those who do.

Concentrating on how to glorify Jesus is like studying a multi-faceted diamond. Simply put, there are many different ways of looking at it and beholding its beauty. You will notice that each of the chapters in this book discusses a particular angle on glorifying Him in our lives — by embracing the divine mindset, by reckoning the paradoxes of the Christ-life, by dying to live, by abiding in Him, and so on. It is truly amazing to see how the New Testament emphasizes the critical importance of magnifying Christ from so many different vantage points.

I can think of no grander theme than Christ's exaltation. He alone is worthy. Ironically though, Christ is glorified only by those fallen men who have been redeemed by His blood *and* who have chosen, by God's grace, to glorify Him as their very purpose for living. This is that subset of believers who have submitted to be conformed to the image of Christ. Though Jesus alone is worthy of glory, He will count *them* worthy of sharing in His future, eternal glory. What a resplendent prospect!

> To you who are troubled rest with us, when the Lord Jesus shall be revealed from heaven with his mighty angels … when he shall come to be glorified in his saints, and to be admired in all them that believe … in that day. 2 Thess. 1:7, 10

> Wherefore also we pray always for you, that our God would count you worthy of this calling, and fulfil all the good pleasure of his goodness, and the work of faith with power: That the name of our Lord Jesus Christ may be glorified in you, and ye in him, according to the grace of our God and the Lord Jesus Christ. 2 Thess. 1:11-12

May we be magnifiers and reflectors of our Lord Jesus Christ, that He might be exalted in and through our lives, and that He might count us worthy to be glorified together with Him.

James S. Hollandsworth
Forest City, North Carolina
December, 2015

Chapter 1

Embracing the Divine Mindset

Ten million dollars was contributed to the New York Philharmonic in 1973 by donor Avery Fisher. In recognition of his generous gift, the orchestra renamed their concert hall, *Avery Fisher Hall*. The name held for more than forty years until 2014, when the orchestra decided to raise funds for renovations to the hall. The New York Philharmonic actually paid fifteen million dollars to the heirs of Avery Fisher for the right to remove his name from the hall so they might be able to rename the venue after a new donor. A man named David Geffen stepped to the plate in a fundraising contest, and he won the right to have the hall named after him for the next generation. He donated one hundred million dollars for the honor![1]

Men love the praise of others. Our human nature inherently desires acclaim, honor, and prestige. We want to be in the limelight. It is a pride problem that goes back to the Garden of Eden. We want to be as gods, despite clear admonitions in the Holy Scriptures that pride goes before destruction (Prov. 16:18) and that God resists the proud (James 4:6). Our Lord also warns that those who exalt themselves will be abased; those who humble themselves will be exalted (Matt. 23:12). Despite these warnings from the Scriptures, even Christians tend to resort to pridefulness and strife. The heart is deceitful above all things, and desperately wicked (Jer. 17:9).

In contrast to the arrogance of man, we marvel that the bona fide God of the universe, the Creator of all things, humbled Himself and left Heaven's glories to take on human flesh. For what purpose did He come? He came to die, of course, to atone for the sins of mankind, but the answer to the question is much grander than that. Let us now unfold God's master plan for the ages as revealed in the Scriptures.

> Let this mind be in you, which was also in Christ Jesus: Who, being in the form of God, thought it not robbery to be equal with God: But made himself of no reputation, and took upon him the form of a servant, and was made in the likeness of men: And being found in fashion as a man, he humbled himself, and became obedient unto death, even the death of the cross. Wherefore God also hath highly exalted him, and given him a name which is above every name: That at the name of Jesus every knee should bow, of things in heaven, and things in earth, and things under the earth; And that every tongue should confess that Jesus Christ is Lord, to the glory of God the Father. Phil. 2:5-11

Marvel at Christ's accomplishments. His self-effacement climaxed in exaltation. One day He will be worshipped by all, regardless of what people do with Him now. Jesus will be eminent. However, He wants us to glorify Him now by making Him preeminent. The prefix *pre* means "before" or "in advance of."

> That in all things he might have the preeminence. Col. 1:18

A king is often referred to as "your eminence" to acknowledge His superiority of position. Christ is magnified and God is glorified when we give Jesus *pre*-eminence, that is, eminence in advance of the day when all will bow to Him. If you will bow to Him *now* as your King, then one day you will rule with Him as His co-heir, and He will be glorified by your ruling. Many saved people do not honor Christ as king of their lives. He is not on the throne within; self is on the throne. Oh yes, they are children of God, but Christ is not being glorified in their lives. Incidentally, that could be the case even in the lives of well-meaning Christians who *think* they are glorifying the Lord when, in reality, they are not.

Christ is magnified when you pursue His eternal purpose, choosing to make Him *pre*-eminent in your life by letting His mind be your mind. To that end, it is imperative to understand Christ's mindset and His eternal purpose for the saints throughout all ages.

Divine Love in Eternity Past

> Who, being in the form of God, thought it not robbery to be equal with God. Phil. 2:6

This is a clear statement of the deity of Christ, referring to the time before His incarnation. The word *form* is not the idea of shape. It is referring to His distinctive nature and character as God.[2] The word *robbery*, in this instance, means a prize to be grasped; something to be held onto."[3] Thus, the idea of this verse is that Christ — before His incarnation — "did not regard His divine equality as a prize which was to be grasped at and retained … but, on the contrary, laid aside the form of God, and took upon Himself the nature of man."[4] That is a remarkable statement!

Imagine God, in eternity past, pondering something we might call the "Grand Plan." Perhaps the Godhead considered the question, "Should we create a universe with multiple galaxies and, in one of those spaces, form planet Earth and make people to populate it?" Undoubtedly, the conversation amongst the Godhead was stimulating, whatever form it may have taken. For in divine wisdom, the triune God already knew the outcome of the Grand Plan long before He ever created it. He knew Lucifer would rebel. He knew Eve would be deceived and disobey God, and Adam would follow in disobedience. He knew man would have to die. He knew a lake of fire would also need to be created for the everlasting punishment of the devil and his angels. He knew the Son, through the Spirit, would need to obtain eternal redemption for mankind. Each member of the Trinity knew the great cost before the plan was ever set in motion.

The Son would have to leave the glories of the eternal realm; empty Himself of His divine prerogatives; take on the constraints of human flesh through the means of virgin birth;

live a sinless life on Earth; then give His life an atonement for man's sin.

> Forasmuch as ye know that ye were not redeemed with corruptible things … But with the precious blood of Christ … Who verily was foreordained before the foundation of the world, but was manifest in these last times for you. 1 Pet. 1:18-20

In the divine conversation, Christ never balked. He never shrank from His divine duty. He never once regarded His divine equality as a prize to be grasped at but, rather, laid aside the form of God, and took upon Himself the nature of man. That is the mind of Christ Jesus, and it is to be our mind.

But why would God do it? Why would Jesus submit to it? Why the willingness to undergo the Grand Plan, knowing the devastating consequences? After all, His omniscient risk assessment had assured him of failure on man's part. Nevertheless, the omniscient One carved out of eternity something we know as time and out of infinity something we know as space. Time, of course, has no bearing on God; neither does space. As a Spirit-being, He transcends space-time, standing outside of its constraints. He can see the beginning and ending of the universe, and everything in between, simultaneously. He knows what has happened and what will happen — "in real time," we might say, tongue-in-cheek.

Despite man's failure, God is assured of success. But again, why would He do it? The answer is profound and beyond our human comprehension, particularly in view of God's foreknowledge. God has conceived a plan by which He will be glorified — and what a marvelous plan it is! The consummation of His plan brings ultimate glory to Him, and to think, we are privileged to play a part, as we shall see.

The second reason I believe God launched the Grand Plan is because of His love and desire for fellowship. One writer put it so eloquently, "God is love, and love cannot live alone."[5] Ponder the endearing prayer of Jesus to His Father while on Earth:

> And the glory which thou gavest me I have given them; that they may be one, even as we are one: I in them, and thou in me, that they may be made perfect in one; and that the world may know that thou hast sent me, and hast loved them, as thou hast loved

me. Father, I will that they also, whom thou hast given me, be with me where I am; that they may behold my glory, which thou hast given me: for thou lovedst me before the foundation of the world. John 17:22-24

Long before the foundation of the world we find divine love, not just amongst the Godhead, but divine love on behalf of the Godhead for mankind that He would create. That's phenomenal! Knowing man would reject Him — the great and Almighty Originator of the universe, who far transcends us — God nevertheless loved us and continues to love us.

And I have declared unto them thy name, and will declare it: that the love wherewith thou hast loved me may be in them, and I in them. John 17:26

Divine love in eternity past is one of the reasons the Godhead was willing to launch the Grand Plan, knowing full well the outcome. What is to be our response back to Him who loved us?

According as he hath chosen us in him before the foundation of the world, that we should be holy and without blame before him in love. Eph. 1:4

Long before He ever created the world, God chose us to holiness and blamelessness before Him *in love*. Some commentators say *in love* modifies His choosing and predestinating. Others say it modifies our holiness and blamelessness, emphasizing that it is to be in love. Perhaps *both* are implied. We know He loved us before the foundation of the world, and in His love, He chose that we should be holy and blameless. It doesn't say He dictated that we would be. It says that we *should*. The Greek scholar Vincent confirms this practical — as opposed to positional — meaning of *holy and without blame*, by saying, "The reference is to *moral* rather than to *forensic* righteousness."[6] In other words, this is not referring to the imputed righteousness of Christ, the legal righteousness we receive at salvation, known as justification. This is experiential, sanctifying righteousness in everyday living, that is, choosing to live righteously. *But as he which hath called you is holy, so be ye holy in all manner of conversation,* 1 Pet. 1:15. It is our *reasonable service*, Rom. 12:1, but how many Christians fail to live holily and blamelessly? Nevertheless, it is God's will; indeed, it is one of His purposes for creating us — that we may be holy and without blame *in love*.

In eternity past — despite knowing in advance the inevitable, devastating outcome of the Grand Plan — God, nevertheless, chose to create man out of His heart of love and desire for fellowship. He did so, knowing full well mankind's need for redemption, necessitating that He lay aside the form of God, and take upon Himself the nature of man. What wondrous love!

> He left His Father's throne above,
> So free, so infinite His grace!
> Emptied Himself of all but love,
> and bled for Adam's helpless race.
> Amazing love! How can it be
> That Thou, my God, shouldst die for me?[7]

As children of God we are instructed, *Let this mind be in you which was also in Christ Jesus*, Phil. 2:5.

Divine Humility in the Present Age

> But made himself of no reputation, and took upon him the form of a servant, and was made in the likeness of men: And being found in fashion as a man, he humbled himself, and became obedient unto death, even the death of the cross. Phil. 2:7-8

Jesus made Himself of no reputation. Literally, He emptied Himself. This is the theological concept referred to as the *kenosis*, based on the Greek word for *no reputation*, the idea of emptying. Of what did He empty Himself? He certainly did not divest Himself of divinity. Jesus was God from eternity past and never ceased to be God, even as He took upon Himself the form of a servant. Of what, then, did He empty Himself? Jesus laid aside His divine prerogatives. Without forfeiting His divine attributes, He simply chose not to use them as a man on Earth so that He could live as God originally intended for man to live, and that is in total dependence on God.

Jesus did everything on Earth *as a man,* in the power of the Holy Spirit, in the same fashion that we are to conduct ourselves in the power of the Holy Spirit. In John 5:19 He said, *The Son can do nothing of Himself,* and again in John 8:38, *I do nothing of myself.* Jesus demonstrated that divine attributes are not necessary for living a life of victory. What is necessary is dependence on the divine life within, the Holy Spirit, the Spirit of Christ. *For without me,* Jesus said, *ye can do nothing,* John 15:5. What an example for us, demonstrating that victory is possible in reliance on the Holy Spirit.

Phil. 2:7 says Christ took upon Him the *form* — the distinctive nature and character — of a man. He willingly took upon Him Man-essence. How so? By submitting to a virgin birth and, as all of us, being born of a human mother. *The Word was made flesh, and dwelt among us,* John 1:14. We call this the incarnation. Here's the bottom line: Christ humbled Himself and showed great restraint by not relying on His divine attributes while on Earth. That is beyond comprehension.

Jesus is God. He is the Creator of the world. He made mankind and possesses all power and wisdom, and He is everywhere present. But He deliberately determined to come to Earth and not use any of His divine power or attributes. The Romans crucified Him at the behest of the Jewish leadership. Nevertheless, He became obedient unto death; He humbly submitted to it. He didn't resist His torturers. He didn't call twelve legions of angels to destroy the Romans and set Himself free. He had the divine ability to right the wrongs and begin ruling as rightful king of this world. He was capable of melting down the earth. But He didn't do it. Meanwhile the bad guy, so to speak, got away with his shenanigans, as least it seemed that way. Jesus restrained Himself, for He chose not to function as God on Earth but as man on Earth, in *everything*.

Again, we are reminded, *Let this mind be in you, which was also in Christ Jesus,* Phil. 2:5. Choose His mindset of love, His mindset of humility.

Divine Glory in the Age to Come

> Wherefore God also hath highly exalted him, and given him a name which is above every name. Phil. 2:9

The wonderful result of Christ's humility is His exaltation. Notice the marvelous phrase, *highly exalted*. Just how highly was He exalted? The apostle Paul answers this question in his prayer for the Ephesians.

> That ye may know ... what is the exceeding greatness of his power to us-ward who believe, according to the working of his mighty power, which he wrought in Christ, when he raised him from the dead, and set him at his own right hand in the heavenly places, far above all principality, and power, and might, and dominion, and every name that is named ... and hath put all things under his feet. Eph. 1:18-22

How highly has Jesus been exalted? He is presently at the right hand of the Father, a place of authority and power. All things are under His feet, and He is *far above all principality, and power, and might, and dominion,* apparent references to the Satanic realm. Jesus, because of His humility and obedience in going to the cross of Calvary, has been exalted *as a man* to the right hand of the Father. Think of it! There is a *man* in Heaven, seated on the throne of God. Jesus has not been divested of His body, nor will He be. He will always be a *man* in the presence of God the Father. Jesus is the God-man.

Don't miss the profound truth of these verses. It is a *man* that is far above the Satanic realm. It could have been Adam, had Adam not sinned. But Adam did sin, and so death was passed to all men, for all have sinned (Rom. 5:12). Jesus came to right the wrongs, to reclaim the kingdom that Adam forfeited to Satan. Jesus, as the second Adam, lived the life that God had intended for the first Adam to live. Not only has Jesus been exalted to the right hand of the Father, a place of authority, He has also been given a name above every name, the name of *Jesus*. His other names are incredible too — *Wonderful, Counsellor, The mighty God, The everlasting Father, The Prince of Peace,* Isa. 9:6. But His name *Jesus* is best of all — better than His other names and certainly better than any other name in Heaven or Earth, because of what it represents.

Jesus already possesses authority, but Jesus is not presently ruling as King. Oh, don't misunderstand. He's *my* king; He's on the throne of *my* heart. I trust He is ruling in your life too. However, He is not ruling in a literal sense, on a throne over a kingdom, per se. But that day is coming, and

Paul reminds us that in that day every knee will bow and every tongue will confess that Jesus Christ is Lord (Phil. 2:10). I believe that applies to both saved and lost and even the spirit realm. One day He will be the eminent, righteous king of the world, and we will reign with Him, that is, those of His faithful ones who qualify to reign with Him.

Even though God has highly exalted Jesus by placing Him at the Father's right hand, the ultimate glorification of Christ is yet to come.

> And that every tongue should confess that Jesus Christ is Lord, to the glory of God the Father. Phil. 2:11

The way multitudes of churches carry out their ministries, you would think the ultimate goal of the Grand Plan is the salvation of mankind. Please don't misunderstand. Salvation in Jesus Christ is critical in the Grand Plan, but it is not the end in itself. It is only the means to the end. The end is when Christ is glorified as millennial King, co-ruling with His faithful bride, when He ultimately casts Satan into the lake of fire at the end of His millennial reign and then turns over His kingdom to the eternal kingdom of God. Only then, in an ultimate sense, will God the Father be glorified.

Thus we can say emphatically that the purpose of the Grand Plan is not merely the salvation of lost people, as important as that is, but the exaltation of Christ, along with the exaltation of the many sons He brings unto glory to rule with Him as co-regents in His coming kingdom (more on that in Chapter 5). **What this means is that we must not stop short at the cross in our philosophy of life and ministry, but go all the way to the future reign of Christ.** To be sure, God is glorified in the crucifixion and resurrection of His Son, Jesus Christ, but if it ends there, it is not enough. The eternal plan conceived in the mind of God only finds its fulfillment when God is ultimately glorified in the millennial ruler and His co-regents.

What, then, is the practical application of these important truths?

Divine Manifestation in the Lives of Saints

1 If there be therefore any consolation in Christ, if any comfort of love, if any fellowship of the Spirit, if any bowels and mercies,
2 Fulfil ye my joy, that ye be likeminded, having the same love, being of one accord, of one mind.
3 Let nothing be done through strife or vainglory; but in lowliness of mind let each esteem other better than themselves.
4 Look not every man on his own things, but every man also on the things of others.
5 Let this mind be in you, which was also in Christ Jesus.
Phil. 2:1-5

Letting Christ's mind be in you means, not only that you have an inward, Christlike spirit of love and humility, as illustrated in the points above, but that those qualities become implemented in your interpersonal relationships.

Verse one begins with the word *if*. Some commentators point out that it could accurately be translated *since*. In other words, *since* there is consolation or encouragement because of our union with Christ; and *since* there is comfort from His love; and *since* there is fellowship or partnership with the Holy Spirit; and *since* there are bowels and mercies, or tenderness and compassion; you should be like-minded, and of one accord and one mind with other believers (v. 2). Nothing should be done contentiously or for self-glory, but rather, choosing lowliness of mind, you must value others better than self (v. 3). Finally, don't look out for your own interests; look out for the interests of others (v. 4). The commands in vs. 2-4 are made possible by the provision in v. 1.

The admonition in v. 5 looks backward to vs. 1-4 and forward to vs. 6-11. You are to choose the mindset of Christ in both respects. In the earlier verses, we find His mindset of love and compassion. He was not contentious but was lowly in mind, looking out for the interests of others. He promoted unity amongst the saints. Let this mind be in you! Choose to think and act in His loving way rather than selfishly. In the later verses, we find His mindset was humble and submissive. He willingly left Heaven's glories, laying aside the use of His divine attributes. He chose to be born of a virgin and take on human flesh. He endured the horrors of crucifixion, willing to suffer for mankind. Let this mind be in you!

It is high time, children of God, that we stop thinking of self and start loving others. It is high time that we submit to the Lordship of Christ in our lives and humble ourselves. Oh, may His mindset be manifest in our mindset, and may He thereby be preeminent in our lives, that Christ might be magnified, and that we might share in His glory in the age to come! May we, together with Him, fulfill the quintessential purpose for which we were created, the ultimate purpose of the Grand Plan: His exaltation.

Be Thou exalted, forever and ever,
God of eternity, the Ancient of Days!
Wondrous in wisdom, majestic in glory,
Perfect in holiness, and worthy of praise.

Be Thou exalted, O Son of the Highest,
Savior of sinful men, Redeemer and King!
One with the Father, co-equal in glory,
Humbly we come to Thee our homage to bring.

Be Thou exalted, O Spirit of power,
Dwelling within our hearts, to keep us from sin.
God of the ages, and Lord of Salvation,
Ruler of heav'n and earth, Thy praises we sing!

Refrain

Be Thou exalted by seraphs and angels,
Be Thou exalted with harp and with song;
Saints in their anthems of rapture adore Thee,
Thine be the glory forever, Amen![8]

---

[1] "David Geffen Hall," *Wikipedia: The Free Encyclopedia* (accessed Dec., 2015).

[2] Marvin R. Vincent, *Word Studies in the New Testament* (Peabody, MA: Hendrickson Publ., no copyright), vol. 3, 430.

[3] John F. Walvoord and Roy B. Zuck, ed., *The Bible Knowledge Commentary: New Testament* (Wheaton, IL: Victor Books, 1983), 654.

[4] Vincent, *Word Studies in the New Testament*, vol. 3, 432.

[5] Ruth Paxson. *The Wealth, Walk and Warfare of the Christian* (Old Tappan, NJ: Fleming H. Revell Co., 1939), 30.

[6] Vincent, *Word Studies in the New Testament*, vol. 3, 365.

[7] Charles Wesley, "And Can It Be That I Should Gain?" (No. 44) in *Great Hymns of the Faith* (Grand Rapids, MI: Singspiration, Inc./Zondervan, 1968).

[8] Fanny J. Crosby, "Be Thou Exalted" (No. 57) in *Rejoice Hymns* (Greenville, SC: Majesty Music, 2011).

Chapter 2

Reckoning the Paradoxes

The watershed event of world history is the resurrection of Jesus Christ. Imagine for a moment the state of Christianity if Christ had not risen from the grave:

- Our sins would not be forgiven (1 Cor. 15:17).
- The serpent would have crushed Messiah's head, not the other way around (Gen. 3:15).
- Satan would be the victor, along with sin and death and hell (1 Cor. 15:55-57; Heb. 2:14).
- There would be no life after death (1 Cor. 15:18).
- Life would be meaningless and hopeless (1 Cor. 15:19).
- Trusting Christ for salvation would be of no avail (1 Cor. 15:14).
- Testifying of Christ would make us deluded, intolerant fanatics — indeed, it would make us liars (1 Cor. 15:15).
- The Word of God would be fraudulent (1 Cor. 15:15).
- Our preaching would be useless, for the gospel would be powerless to save (1 Cor. 15:14).

Thankfully, Jesus rose again from the grave.

> But now is Christ risen from the dead, and become the firstfruits of them that slept. For since by man came death, by man came also the resurrection of the dead. For as in Adam all die, even so in Christ shall all be made alive. 1 Cor. 15:20-22

Hallelujah! Though Adam brought sin and death into this world, Jesus brought forgiveness and life. Because Christ was resurrected, we will one day be resurrected. That is profound truth, but equally significant is that His resurrection life can be ours *now*, in an experiential sense, even in this present age. Incidentally, that is what God desires for all of His children, as it is the only life that will please Him and magnify His holy name.

Living His Resurrected Life

Christ's resurrection demands a choice on our part. It is a very critical choice to live His resurrected life. For what you do with the resurrection determines whether or not Christ is glorified in your life — both now and eternally. In other words, there are serious consequences to your decision.

> If ye then be risen with Christ, seek those things which are above, where Christ sitteth on the right hand of God. Set your affection on things above, not on things on the earth. For ye are dead, and your life is hid with Christ in God. When Christ, who is our life, shall appear, then shall ye also appear with him in glory. Col. 3:1-4

> According to my earnest expectation and my hope, that in nothing I shall be ashamed, but that with all boldness, as always, so now also Christ shall be magnified in my body, whether it be by life, or by death. For to me to live is Christ, and to die is gain. Phil. 1:20-21

Generally speaking, believers have two opportunities for magnifying Christ: in life, and in death. You can live in such a manner that He is glorified by your life, and you can die in such a manner that you honor Him, magnifying Him in the act of dying as well as by the legacy you leave behind. It is pointing others to Him by your life and by your death, so that He increases as you decrease. The philosophy of a life lived in this fashion is summed up well in Phil. 1:21, *To live is Christ, and to die is gain*. Living is about Jesus, and dying is to His gain as well. Of course, dying with this mindset is also gain because at that point our union with Him is complete. Either way — living or dying — is a win-win situation.

Earnest expectation "describes straining one's neck to catch a glimpse of something that is ahead."[9] Paul was clearly fixated on the future and pleasing Christ. That was His intense anticipation. He wanted to meet Jesus and hear the words, *well done.* To that end, He recognized the necessity of living boldly and unashamed for Jesus and He wanted to die in the same manner. His driving passion was that Christ be magnified whether Paul was living or dying, and that should drive us as well. But unfortunately, multitudes of saints are not consumed with magnifying Christ. It seems they are more content to magnify self.

Christ is magnified when you live the resurrected life of victory, so that your behavior makes Jesus appear more glorious to others. The apostle Paul referred to this as the Christ-life.

> I am crucified with Christ: nevertheless I live; yet not I, but Christ liveth in me: and the life which I now live in the flesh I live by the faith of the Son of God, who loved me, and gave himself for me. Gal. 2:20

Notice the three paradoxes in this single verse of Scripture.

The Paradox of Crucifixion

I am crucified with Christ: nevertheless I live. What a seeming contradiction of words! I died with Christ, but I live. How do we resolve the paradox of crucifixion? The key is understanding that when you died with Him, you were also raised with Him. The paradox is solved by seeing that resurrection follows crucifixion; life follows death. How critical for our understanding.

There is not one saint who can claim, "I died for my sins." Nor can anyone say, "I helped Christ to die for my sins." All we can say is what the apostle Paul proclaimed in 1 Cor. 15:3, *Christ died for our sins.* The point here is that being crucified with Christ in no way suggests *you* did something. He did it all. Yet, how remarkable for our text to say we are crucified *with Christ.* What does that mean?

God is telling us what happened spiritually when we became children of God. At that point, a transaction occurred. Through salvation, His physical death became our spiritual death. We died *with Him*. We were crucified *with Him*. But let us not misunderstand. We are not crucified with Christ *for* our sin. There is nothing we can do to help Christ pay *for* our sin. Jesus paid it all. We are crucified with Him *unto* our sin. That speaks to the wonderful deathblow Christ dealt to sin's power on our behalf.

> For in that he died, he died unto sin once ... Likewise reckon ye also yourselves to be dead indeed unto sin, but alive unto God through Jesus Christ our Lord. Rom. 6:10-11

As a result, we are *dead to sin*, Rom. 6:2.

> Therefore we are buried with him by baptism into death: that like as Christ was raised up from the dead by the glory of the Father, even so we also should walk in newness of life. Rom. 6:4

When Christ died, you died with Him. It is as if you were buried with Him by baptism — not referring here directly to water baptism, although water baptism is a wonderful picture of this spiritual transaction. The word *baptism* simply means immersion. You were immersed in His death, which implies burial, and then you were raised in His resurrection. Because of that, you have two benefits, according to this text.

Benefit #1: You walk in newness of life

The old master of sin and death has gone, never to return. The new master of righteousness and life (Jesus) has arrived, never to leave. That wonderful transaction happened in your *spirit* at the moment of your salvation. You already possess it. According to 1 John 3:9, God's seed (Greek, *sperma*) remains in you, and you do not continue sinning in the realm of your *spirit* because you have been born of God. You have been justified — made completely righteous (2 Cor. 5:21) — in your *spirit*, and you have been positionally sanctified — made completely holy in your *spirit* (Heb. 10:10).

> Knowing this, that our old man is crucified with him, that the body of sin might be destroyed, that henceforth we should not serve sin. Rom. 6:6

Your old man — your old master — is dead. You are a completely new creature in Christ (2 Cor. 5:17). Because of that, you have a second benefit.

Benefit #2: Sin is powerless to rule over you

Notice the phrase *body of sin* in v. 6 above. It is not referring to your physical body, and it is not referring to your old man. Your old man died, and dead things can't come back to life unless Christ enlivens them, and He's not about to enliven your old man. The body of sin is the flesh principle that continues to dwell in your *soul*, as distinct from your *spirit*. It is the power of sin in your life that keeps tugging on you to pursue evil rather than righteousness.

> I find then a law, that, when I would do good, evil is present with me … But I see another law in my members, warring against the law of my mind, and bringing me into captivity to the law of sin which is in my members. Rom. 7:21,23

Paul also described the body of sin in v. 20 as *sin that dwelleth in me*. This is not the same thing as your old man or old master in the realm of your *spirit*. He died; that's what crucifixion with Christ did to him. This is the flesh principle or power of sin that continues in your *soul* even after you are saved. That is why you still sin.

But the glorious benefit is that the flesh principle no longer has power to rule you. It has been *destroyed*. The word does not mean "annihilated." It means "rendered powerless." It is the same word used in Heb. 2:14. Jesus *destroyed* the devil. Jesus didn't kill Satan and annihilate him. He rendered Satan powerless through the crucifixion and resurrection. In like manner Jesus rendered the flesh principle within you powerless to control you.

> For he that is dead is freed from sin. Rom. 6:7

> For sin shall not have dominion over you. Rom. 6:14

A dead man no longer has to pay taxes; he no longer has to keep the law. He is freed from these things on account of his death. So followers of Christ are free from the *power* of sin, for we have been crucified with Christ. Of course, we are also free from the *penalty* of sin, but that is the subject matter of chapter five of Romans, not chapter six.

Sin is powerless to rule you! You are free from sin's power. But you may wonder: Why do I keep sinning? It is because you are *allowing* sin to rule you. It may be that you have not reckoned the truth of Rom. 6.

> Likewise reckon ye also yourselves to be dead indeed unto sin, but alive unto God through Jesus Christ our Lord. Rom. 6:11

Reckon

The word *reckon* is an accounting term. It means to take inventory and then regard it as accurate. To reckon yourself as *dead indeed unto sin, but alive unto God through Jesus Christ* is to be convinced of this truth. But it's not mere intellectual assent. That is where multitudes of Christians fall short of finding true victory in their spiritual lives. They have read this truth and know it to be true because it is in the Word of God. But they don't take it by faith.

Perhaps that applies to you. You are trying to make this truth a reality by doing things. You try to die with Christ by eradicating those things from your life that displease the Lord. You try to rise with Christ by doing those things that please Him. Nevertheless, you have been unsuccessful, or you have convinced yourself of a substandard definition of success. Perhaps you have rationalized your spiritual condition as normal when in reality God calls it abnormal. You have missed the key to unlocking this truth.

If you are a child of God, you are *already* dead to sin. Indeed, you died with Christ. A transaction occurred in your spirit the day you were saved. Furthermore, you are *already* risen with Him, which means you are alive unto God. That transaction also occurred in your spirit when you were saved. Thus, you are *already*, *officially* dead to sin and alive unto God through Christ. It's a done deal. You cannot become "more dead" or "more alive." So believe it. Reckoning is the idea of not only understanding it intellectually but also embracing it in your affections and choosing to depend on this truth.

Reckon that your *spirit* is now completely righteous, and your new master now lives there. His name is Holy Spirit. Your *spirit* is completely new, for it has been saved, justified, and positionally sanctified by Jesus.

But your *soul* still has vestiges of the old life — does it not? When you got saved, your thoughts were not completely erased and made new. Your feelings were not re-geared and made new. No, in your *soul*, you have the same propensities to sin because of the flesh principle or the power of sin. But the truth to be understood and believed is that it has been rendered powerless because the old master is gone and the new master has moved in. Reckon! Now that you are saved, you have to learn to submit to the new master, not to indwelling sin.

The first paradox of crucifixion / resurrection is followed by a second paradox in Gal. 2:20.

The Paradox of Exchange

Yet not I, but Christ liveth in me. Your life exchanged for His life. Here's the paradox of exchange: When you give Him *your* life, He gives you *His* life. This exchange is possible because the day you were saved, Christ moved into your life, through His Holy Spirit.

> What? know ye not that your body is the temple of the Holy Ghost which is in you, which ye have of God, and ye are not your own?
> 1 Cor. 6:19

Imagine that! Deity lives within you. Now put yourself in the shoes of the apostles who, during their years with Jesus, were not indwelt by the Holy Spirit. They walked with Jesus for three years, saw Him heal the sick, cast out demons, bring calm to stormy seas, rebuke the Pharisees, preach powerful messages, provide comfort and encouragement, raise Lazarus, and even live a sinless life. Then He announced He was going away. What heartache and agony it must have been for the disciples to hear this. Jesus had been their dear friend, the kindest, most loving person they had ever met, who had never sinned. In fact, Jesus went so far as to tell them it was expedient (profitable) that He leave. The men must have surely thought, "How can this be?" To them, His comment seemed inexplicable. But Jesus went on to explain that unless He were to leave, the Holy Spirit would not come.

The implication is that the indwelling presence of the omnipresent Holy Spirit — who resides with every believer on a 24/7 basis — is so much better than the limited presence of Jesus as a man. The Spirit enables greater works. Though they probably could not comprehend these things at the time Jesus said them, they surely understood after the Spirit came to indwell each of them permanently.

Consider the ramifications for modern saints. The Holy Spirit lives within each of us and manifests the life of Christ in us — not an imitation of Christ, but Christ Himself. When the self-life dies, then the Christ-life lives. This happens whenever the believer surrenders self and chooses to depend on Christ for enablement. Remember, Jesus never lied, lusted, worried, coveted, cursed, or became frustrated or annoyed. To the extent that Christ's life is our life, neither will we. What a paradox, because we know ourselves!

> For I know that in me (that is, in my flesh,) dwelleth no good thing. Rom. 7:18

Nevertheless, when Christ is living His life through yours, the result is always a very good thing. As we already learned, you have every provision to live victoriously over sin. You don't have to be defeated by sin. Why, then, do you continue to sin, knowing that sin is powerless to rule you (Rom. 6:14)? If sin is ruling you, then you have not exchanged your life for His life. That's a tragedy, for the Holy Spirit of God who lives within you is eager to enable you to obey God. It is as if the key to your jail cell is hanging on a hook just outside the door, within your reach. Your failure to use the key of promise to unlock the door of sin's imprisonment is your own choice.

> That the righteousness of the law might be fulfilled in us, who walk not after the flesh, but after the Spirit. For they that are after the flesh do mind the things of the flesh; but they that are after the Spirit the things of the Spirit. Rom. 8:4-5

Have you made the exchange? Have you yielded your flesh to His Spirit so that Christ's life is made manifest in your life? How does one do this?

> Neither yield ye your members as instruments of unrighteousness unto sin: but yield yourselves unto God, as those that are alive from the dead, and your members as instruments of righteousness unto God. Rom. 6:13

Yield to God

The word *yield* means to surrender. The same Greek word is translated *present* in Rom. 12:1. It is interesting that in Rom. 14:10 it is translated *stand before* in the verse, *We shall all stand before the judgment seat of Christ*. That is, we will all yield at the Judgment Seat. Perhaps surrendering is best illustrated by a white flag on the battlefield. It is a symbol, conveying the message, "We give over ourselves to the will of the other." Yielding to God is seeing yourself as totally incapable of winning the battle against sin and raising the white flag in humility to God as if to say, "I cannot win; I give this over to you. Please enable me to find the victory."

> But thanks be to God, which giveth us the victory through our Lord Jesus Christ. 1 Cor. 15:57

Yielding is a moment-by-moment decision to let Him take control of your life as you die to self. It is letting Him have His way rather than you having yours. Yielding is exchanging your flesh for His Spirit. When the Spirit of Christ is reigning on the throne of your life, there will be victory over sin. You will be abiding in the vine, manifesting the fruit of the Spirit. Incidentally, God will not force you to submit to Him. But He desires that you voluntarily surrender all on a daily basis. Paul said, *I die daily*, 1 Cor. 15:31.

The world spews out the philosophy, "You are in control of your own life; let no one be your master; take control and experience real living." On the contrary, God says, "Yield to me and you will live." When your life is exchanged for His life, the result is beautiful. Marvel at the glorious benefits:

> But now being made free from sin, and become servants to God, ye

have your fruit unto holiness, and the end everlasting life. Rom. 6:22

That the righteousness of the law might be fulfilled in us, who walk not after the flesh, but after the Spirit. Rom. 8:4

Yet not I, but Christ liveth in me. That is the paradox of exchange. A third paradox is found in Gal. 2:20.

The Paradox of Dependence

The life which I now live in the flesh I live by faith. Why is this considered a paradox? We presently live in a human body, which is confined by space and time, limited by its senses. It wants to believe only what it can see and hear and smell and taste and touch. In contrast, living by faith is living in complete dependence on God, not in dependence on our human senses — even though we cannot see Him or hear Him or feel Him in a sensory way. The paradox of dependence is that when you stop depending on yourself, and start depending on Him, He will give you victory.

Faith enables us to see the invisible things of eternity, the realm our senses cannot experience. Faith enables us to live eternity *now*. What is faith? As already implied, it is dependence on God. How can one, through faith, experience the eternal realm in this present world? The apostle Paul gives a classic illustration in his personal testimony.

We are troubled on every side, yet not distressed; we are perplexed, but not in despair; Persecuted, but not forsaken; cast down, but not destroyed; Always bearing about in the body the dying of the Lord Jesus, that the life also of Jesus might be made manifest in our body. 2 Cor. 4:8-10

How can anyone have this attitude? The answer is found in later verses:

13 We having the same spirit of faith, according as it is written, I believed, and therefore have I spoken; we also believe, and therefore speak;
14 Knowing that he which raised up the Lord Jesus shall raise up us also by Jesus, and shall present us with you.
15 For all things are for your sakes, that the abundant grace might

through the thanksgiving of many redound to the glory of God.
16 For which cause we faint not; but though our outward man
perish, yet the inward man is renewed day by day.
17 For our light affliction, which is but for a moment, worketh for
us a far more exceeding and eternal weight of glory;
18 While we look not at the things which are seen, but at the things
which are not seen: for the things which are seen are temporal; but
the things which are not seen are eternal. 2 Cor. 4:13-18

The Same Spirit of Faith

Though on the outside Paul was facing intense persecution
and hardship, on the inside he was rejoicing, for he was being
renewed daily. The apostle's soul was focused, not on the
temporal and physical, but on the unseen and eternal. The key
to having this attitude is faith, described in v. 13. In fact, he
describes it as *the same spirit of faith*. What is meant by *same*?
Paul is quoting Ps. 116, so he wants to have the same spirit of
faith as exemplified by the psalmist.

> 3 The sorrows of death compassed me, and the pains of hell gat
> hold upon me: I found trouble and sorrow.
> 4 Then called I upon the name of the LORD; O LORD, I beseech
> thee, deliver my soul.
> 6 The LORD preserveth the simple: I was brought low, and he
> helped me.
> 8 For thou hast delivered my soul from death, mine eyes from
> tears, and my feet from falling.
> 10 I believed, therefore have I spoken. Ps. 116: 3-4, 6, 8, 10a

That same spirit of faith is also available to you, child of
God, if you will depend on Him, as did the psalmist and Paul
the apostle. Faith is recognizing your own inability and helplessness, choosing to rely on Him. That is how the exchange is
made from your life to His life.

A Personal Testimony

Early in my pastoral ministry I came to a crisis. I could not
seem to get victory in my personal life over some besetting
sins and my ministry seemed powerless. I could relate to the
apostle Paul's heart cry in Rom. 7 (paraphrase), "The things I
don't want to do I keep doing, and the things I want to do I

can't seem to do. Oh wretched man! Who shall deliver me from this body of death?"

I was trying hard to serve the Lord, and when times of defeat would come along, I would try a little harder. Therein was the problem. I was throwing self-effort at my failure in greater measure, always thinking I could conquer and win. Sure, I asked the Lord for help, but I did not realize at the time that even my prayer was self-focused — asking for His help so that I could be successful and achieve something of importance in my ministry. I was not completely dependent on the Lord for enablement to be victorious for His glory.

In my self-inflicted pain, I wondered, "Isn't there something more than this?" Indeed, there was, but I wasn't experiencing it at the time, nor did I know if it really existed. I accepted constant struggle as the norm in my personal life and ministry. Isn't that what others were experiencing too? In my longing for "something more," and at the end of my rope, I cried out sincerely and with no shred of trying to help out God, "Lord, help me! My heart wants to serve you, but I cannot seem to get lasting victory." God graciously heard my cry and answered through His Word. He directed my attention to a verse of Scripture that became the subject of extended meditation.

> But he giveth more grace. Wherefore he saith, God resisteth the proud, but giveth grace unto the humble. James 4:6

I did not fully understand what God was trying to tell me. Was I proud? I didn't think so at the time, but that verse hammered away at my heart for months until God graciously shined through to reveal the form of my pride: self-effort. The Holy Spirit illumined the Word and my spiritual lights came on. My failure to depend on Him alone for victory was negating His grace. It was my own foolish pride, and it resulted in God resisting my efforts.

I used to think that conquering sin was a gradual process of rooting out weeds in my spiritual garden, requiring continual effort on my part to conquer habits and form new ones — with God's help, of course! No matter how hard I tried, the weeds kept popping up, choking out the fruit of my labors. My striving to keep up with the garden was toilsome and never-ending. Needless to say, I never experienced a "victory garden," and soon became weary in well-doing. I eventually learned the metaphor was wrong.

The Lord used a series of questions to change my old paradigm.

> Received ye the Spirit by the works of the law, or by the hearing of faith? Are ye so foolish? having begun in the Spirit, are ye now made perfect by the flesh? Gal. 3:2-3

What an awakening! I had been saved by God's grace through faith alone, with no meritorious effort on my part. However, my Christian life had been characterized by striving and "trying harder" in order to get victory over sin. Yet, those are the building blocks of self-effort. I had been foolish, attempting to make myself "perfect" by the flesh, keeping my list of things that I thought were making me spiritual. But they weren't. On the contrary, they were nullifying God's grace in my life.

> As ye have therefore received Christ Jesus the Lord, so walk ye in him. Col. 2:6

I received Him by faith. Why hadn't I been walking by faith, in total dependence on God?

Christ offers to free sinners from the *penalty* of sin if they will come to Him in faith alone. In like manner, He offers to free saints from the *power* of sin if they will come to Him in faith alone. Just as any degree of effort at the point of conversion keeps an unbeliever from becoming saved, so any degree of effort at the point of reckoning keeps a believer from becoming victorious over sin. Have you accepted Christ's first offer? Then what about the second offer?

The beauty of the dependent life is that when we rely on God in utter helplessness, He delivers us from the flesh. The result is beautiful:

> There is therefore now no condemnation to them which are in Christ Jesus, who walk not after the flesh, but after the Spirit. For the law of the Spirit of life in Christ Jesus hath made me free from the law of sin and death. For what the law could not do, in that it was weak through the flesh, God sending his own Son in the

likeness of sinful flesh, and for sin, condemned sin in the flesh: **That the righteousness of the law might be fulfilled in us, who walk not after the flesh, but after the Spirit**. Rom. 8:1-4

We can live righteously! The Bible says so. We don't have to live in constant defeat. Indeed, a defeated struggle is abnormal in the Christian life, though we have grown to accept it as the norm in Christianity because of our anemic experience. The key to victory is depending on Christ for the enabling grace to let His life be lived in ours. We access His grace by faith.

By whom also we have access by faith into this grace wherein we stand, and rejoice in hope of the glory of God. Rom. 5:2

Take Up Your Cross

One day as I was driving along the interstate, I noticed along the side of the road a small cross in the grass with some flowers around it and on the cross, a name inscribed. Apparently, someone had lost a loved one in a vehicle accident at that very place, and that was their way of remembering and honoring. But the blessed paradox of Gal. 2:20 is that in a spiritual sense we should have many such crosses along the road of life, signaling the daily death of self. We should be able to look back and remember numerous crosses, signifying all the times we died to self by choosing to depend on Christ so that He might live through us. What a joy those crosses bring, as they represent dying so that we might truly live. Learn the paradoxes of the Christ-life:

* The paradox of Crucifixion — Reckon that sin is powerless to rule you.
* The paradox of Exchange — Trade your life for His life.
* The paradox of Dependence — Receive His enabling grace by faith.

[9] Walvoord, *The Bible Knowledge Commentary*, 651.

Chapter 3

Dying to Live

The night I preached at the Bowery Rescue Mission in Manhattan, I could not help but notice the words taped to the pulpit, *Sirs, we would see Jesus.* What a challenge to any preacher of the Word of God! Those special words were first uttered by a group of Greek proselytes who were attending the Passover feast in Jerusalem and approached Christ's disciples, seeking an audience with Jesus (John 12:21).

We would see Jesus was their request. It was not a demand, but a polite longing for personal exposure so they could learn more about Him. The text implies they desired fellowship with the Christ and wanted to learn more of His teachings. These were sincere men, in contrast to the Pharisees. Thus, Jesus took time to teach them about discipleship. What He said must have surprised these Gentiles, for He made them a costly proposition. Indeed, it is a proposition to be considered by any believer of any era.

> And Jesus answered them, saying, The hour is come, that the Son of man should be glorified. Verily, verily, I say unto you, Except a corn of wheat fall into the ground and die, it abideth alone: but if it die, it bringeth forth much fruit. John 12:23-24

Consider the Grain Principle

Christ utters these words in Jerusalem, just hours before His crucifixion. He knows the time has come for Him to be offered as the Lamb of God for the sins of the world. He will, like a seed, go into the ground and die with the prospect of being raised and becoming glorified, bringing forth much fruit. He applies this imagery not only to Himself, but also urges anyone who would progress in discipleship to submit to the same in a spiritual sense.

Christ is magnified when you choose to go into the ground and die, when self is put to death in a spiritual sense. The result is glorious fruit-bearing.

The grain principle can be reduced to a three-word statement: *Death precedes harvest*. Before fruit comes forth, the seed must go into the ground and die. Jesus is using an agricultural analogy that can be imagined by anyone.

If I am intending to grow some type of crop, I must plant seed. I may have an entire barn full of seed, but if I never plant it, I will never have any crop, and I will never be able to reap a harvest. I must not eat the seed. I must not grind it into flour and make bread. I must plant it. The seed must be sacrificed if it is to be of value — "buried" in the earth and covered over so that it can "die" and then be "resurrected" to produce new life. For inherent within that little, insignificant grain seed is life — abundant life — that will not be unleashed unless it is buried.

Of course, the planting of just one seed has a multiplied effect. My one seed does not merely produce one more grain seed. It produces multiple grain seeds, and the more seeds that are sown, the more multiplied will be the effect.

The grain seed that is planted always produces like grain. Wheat produces wheat; corn produces corn, and so on. Wheat seeds will never produce corn or vice versa. We understand these basic laws of nature. The seed must be planted or, we could say, buried; it must die, so to speak. Then it will produce much fruit, of the same kind as planted.

The grain principle applies to Christ *and* to His disciples, and that includes us by extension. Jesus desires to be glorified so the Father will be glorified. *The hour is come, that the Son of man should be glorified … Father, glorify thy name*, vs. 23, 28. For Jesus to be glorified, He must be resurrected and exalted to the right hand of the Father. But according to the grain principle, what must happen first? The seed must die. Jesus must suffer and be put to death and then buried. That must happen in order for the seed to germinate and bear fruit. Jesus must die before He can be resurrected and produce many disciples. Because of His death, multitudes from every kindred and tongue and people and nation will be saved. The death of Christ results in a great harvest.

What does the grain principle mean for the disciples of Jesus? The death to which Jesus had to submit in a *physical* sense is the death to which His disciples must submit in a *spiritual* sense if they would bear fruit. This is taking the positional truth explained in the previous chapter, *Reckoning the Paradoxes*, and applying it in a practical sense in your everyday living. It is drawing upon your provision and putting it into practice by the enabling power of the Holy Spirit.

You are called upon to serve Christ, but the effectiveness of your service is not determined merely by how much you do or how busy you remain. Your effectiveness of service for Christ is determined by whether or not you choose to die spiritually. This is uncomfortable, because it is painful. The thought of dying is not a very exciting thought.

What if you choose not to die? Then you will abide alone, according to John 12:24. When you stand before Jesus you will have nothing to show. He may ask, "Where is your fruit?" You may answer: "Lord, I stayed busy for you. I taught a Sunday School class. I was a deacon. I served as a pastor or missionary or on the staff of a Bible college. I kept busy for you!" Nevertheless, busyness will not suffice as rationale at the Judgment Seat. You will have no fruit to show Him worthy of inheriting the kingdom, no unbelievers who were saved because of your witness, no believers who were impacted by your service to live in a manner worthy of inheriting the kingdom — or very few. You will stand before Christ alone and ashamed.

Under this scenario, imagine standing alone at the Judgment Seat of Christ. What an awful, lonely judgment it will be! The works of your flesh will be consumed and nothing will remain, nothing of value, nothing that meets the Savior's approval. Perhaps you think the Christian life is all about *doing*, but Jesus clarifies that it's about *dying!*

Why is the grain principle so powerful? What is the secret? When you die, then self gets out of the way so that Christ can live His life through you. His life is the only life that can produce fruit. You are totally incapable of producing fruit. Staying busy for Christ will only wear you out; it won't produce fruit. But your death removes the one and only obstacle standing in the way of Christ blossoming out from within. Your spiritual death opens the floodgates of the resurrected life of Christ, which is the life that wins, the life that is victorious, the life of harvest. Oh, consider the grain principle!

Consider the Great Cost

> Now is my soul troubled; and what shall I say? Father, save me from this hour: but for this cause came I unto this hour. John 12:27

For Jesus, the great cost is the horror of the cross, the agony of suffering, the cruel shame and reproach. Jesus is facing great consternation of soul. His agony is being fully revealed, but He is not questioning what He should do. He is merely expressing the deep revulsion of His soul toward the cross, particularly the overwhelming aspect of bearing the sins of the world and being forsaken by God.

This expresses the human heart of Jesus. It demonstrates that He was in all points tested like we are, yet without sin (Heb. 4:15). Yet, His resolve is unshaken. He chooses to fulfill the will of the Father. *For this cause came I unto this hour: Father, glorify thy name, vs. 27-28.* In other words, despite the revolting path ahead, He willingly chooses to die. That must be the choice of every disciple as well: "Lord, the suffering may be overwhelming at times as I serve you, but come what may, I choose to die. I want you to be glorified by living your life through me." What does it mean *to die*?

> He that loveth his life shall lose it; and he that hateth his life in this world shall keep it unto life eternal. John 12:25

Thus it becomes clear that *dying* in v. 24 is the same as *hating your life* in v. 25. *Not dying* is the same as *loving your life* in v. 25. The word *life* is used three times in this verse. The first two times refer to our lower, earthly life. But the third time is a different Greek word and it refers to our higher life, our divine life. If you love the lower life, then when you meet Christ at the Judgment Seat, ready to enter the higher life, all you lived for on Earth will be *lost* (the word means "destroyed"). It will burn up in God's testing furnace. *The fire shall try every man's work of what sort it is,* 1 Cor. 3:13.

On the other hand, if you hate the lower life, then when you meet Christ at the Judgment Seat, all you lived for on Earth will be *kept* (the word means "preserved") for eternity. That is, you will reap the benefits throughout eternity. Without a doubt, passages like this teach that how we live our lives now determines the extent to which we will enjoy the blessings of eternity. Yes, all saved people are eternally secure. But all saved people will not experience the same level of blessing in the millennial kingdom or in eternity. In fact, the millennium will be rather miserable for those who love their lives now. They will consciously regret having lived for self rather than dying to self. That is a truth we ought to take seriously.

Knowing, then, that *dying* in v. 24 is the same as *hating your life* in v. 25, what does it mean to *hate your life*? It means to renounce your self-life and endure suffering for Him. It means not to value the things of this world. The bottom line: It means to abhor, despise and forsake anything that keeps you from dying.

George Muller, that great nineteenth century Christian who was a powerful prayer warrior and trusted God for the impossible, was asked the secret of his service for Christ. He replied,

> There was a day when I died, utterly died — died to George Muller, his opinions, preferences, tastes, and will — died to the world, its approval or censure — died to the approval or blame even of my brethren or friends — and since then I have studied only to show myself approved unto God.[10]

Christian, do you hate your life or do you love it? That is a haunting question. If you love it, then you haven't died, and you are not bearing fruit. If you hate your life, then you have died and you are bringing forth much fruit. Death precedes harvest, and when there is harvest, there is a glorious entrance into the kingdom.

Consider the Glorious Benefits

> Father, glorify thy name. Then came there a voice from heaven, saying, I have both glorified it, and will glorify it again. John 12:28

For Jesus, the glorious benefit is that the Father is glorified in the sufferings and death of His Son. The Father is glorified in the resurrection of Jesus.

> Wherefore God also hath highly exalted him, and given him a name which is above every name: That at the name of Jesus every knee should bow, of things in heaven, and things in earth, and things under the earth. Phil. 2:9-10

What are the glorious benefits for Christ's disciples who choose to die spiritually?

1. *If it die, it bringeth forth much fruit,* v. 24b. You will produce much fruit; fruit that remains; the fruit of good works at the Judgment Seat; the fruit of the Spirit; the fruit of lost people getting saved because of your witness; the fruit of a godly legacy and reputation; the fruit of lives impacted for Jesus.
2. *He that hateth his life in this world shall keep it unto life eternal,* v. 25b. You will keep your life (Greek, *psyche,* soul) at the Judgment Seat. Your works will not be burned up. Your soul will be preserved for the millennial age and the eternal world to follow.
3. *Where I am, there shall also my servant be,* v. 26a. You will experience the presence of Christ in a real and practical way. I believe this promise has a present application as well as future. That is, those who choose to die spiritually will enjoy fellowship with Christ now and will also be ensured of remaining in His immediate presence in eternity. They will rule and reign with Him.
4. *If any man serve me, him will my Father honor,* v. 26b. You

will be honored by God the Father. To be *honored* means to be prized and certainly goes along with the idea of being rewarded.

5. *I, if I be lifted up from the earth, will draw all men unto me* (v. 32). Jesus was lifted up in His crucifixion and resurrection. By extension, when we bear in our body the dying of the Lord Jesus, and thereby die to self, His life is made manifest in our body (2 Cor. 4:10). He is then lifted up and exalted in the world — His gospel goes forth. He draws all men to Himself, not *all* in the sense that everyone will be saved, but *all* in the sense that everyone is welcome — men and women, Jews and Gentiles. If you choose not to die, then Christ will not be lifted up to the multitudes that so desperately need Him.

Death precedes harvest. The cost is great, but the benefits are glorious.

Adoniram Judson, the great missionary to Burma, was at the lowest point in his life and ministry after two years of imprisonment and torture, followed by the death of his wife and his third child. With very few results to show for his labor, and facing severe depression, Judson ventured out into the jungle, heartbroken, and built a hut. He gave away nearly all his earthly possessions and lived alone in the hut, with his Bible, to find comfort from the Lord. Instead, He found indictment by the Holy Spirit.

Judson soon came to realize that his own heart was a "loathsome sepulchre," as he described it. He had been fleshly in his motivations, wanting to make a name for himself in Burma. He was plagued by self-love and self-gratification in his ministry. God was doing a work of purging in this man's life.

He decided to dig a grave next to his hut, and he sat beside it for days, staring at it, thinking of his inner corruption and his need to die to self. I suspect Judson got hold of John 12:24, *Except a corn of wheat fall into the ground and die, it abideth alone: but if it die, it bringeth forth much fruit.* He spent another forty days in solitary meditation on the Word of God, seeking answers, eating very little food.

Sitting next to that grave, Judson realized his need and

chose to die spiritually. There he renounced his self-love and self-focus. Out of his "grave" rose a new, humble man that God could use. When Judson finally came out of the jungle, he was indeed a different man — encouraged and seeking to show Christ's love to the people of Burma.

The glorious result was a life that brought forth much fruit thereafter. Folks began to be saved, and Burma was transformed with the gospel. Also, unbeknownst to Judson at the time, one of his converts, a former murderer whose life had been marvelously changed by the Gospel, was now off in a remote part of the jungles evangelizing his people, the Karen tribes of Burma. He went from village to village, and nearly every time he preached many people were saved. The harvest had begun.[11]

Today there is a huge Christian population in Burma because of Judson. I wonder what would have happened had Judson never died next to that grave. Had Judson instead chosen to wallow in self-pity, the precious people of Burma may never have learned of Christ. The land may have plunged further and further into paganism. But a man died, the seed of his life was buried, and his life brought forth much fruit. Are you willing to die, so that Jesus might bring forth fruit from your life?

---

[10] A.T. Pierson, *George Muller of Bristol* (Grand Rapids, MI: Kregel Publications, 1999), 367.

[11] Courtney Anderson, *To the Golden Shore* (Valley Forge, PA: Judson Press, 1987), sections summarized and adapted.

Chapter 4

Abiding in the Vine

Jesus used the familiar imagery of a vineyard, with its verdant beauty and lush grapes, as the backdrop for illustrating the importance of abiding in Christ. His disciples would have quickly grasped the concept of vine and branches, as grapes were prominent in the Middle East in their day.

> Abide in me, and I in you. As the branch cannot bear fruit of itself, except it abide in the vine; no more can ye, except ye abide in me. John 15:4

Some commentators suggest that Jesus and His disciples may have left the upper room, where they had just observed the last supper, and they were headed toward the Garden of Gethsemane. They would likely be observing grape vines along the route. Christ perhaps points to the vines as an object lesson for teaching His disciples. Though we live in the twenty-first century, these words are as much for us as they were for the original disciples of the first century. We are extensions of those men, the fruit of their labors in the Lord. Christ commands us all to *abide* in Him.

Meaning of Abiding

> I am the true vine, and my Father is the husbandman. John 15:1

Jesus uses a beautiful analogy. He likens Himself to a grape vine, and God the Father to the husbandman (vine-dresser). We — that is, children of God — are the branches. Jesus is speaking to saved people, and He calls us to discipleship in verse 4: *Abide in me*. He goes on to explain. Just as a branch cannot bear fruit by itself — it must be attached to the vine and draw its sustenance and life-giving properties from the vine — so we are unable to bear fruit of ourselves. We must abide in Christ if we would bear fruit, and God is glorified when we bear much fruit. But to do so, we must be connected to the vine, which is the source of vitality.

Christ is magnified when you abide in Him and thereby bear much fruit.

What, then, does it mean *to abide*? It means "to stay or remain." The command implies continuing action. To stay or remain implies that you must not leave. You must stay put in the vine if you would bear fruit. Notice in v. 4 the little phrase *in Me* after the word *abide*. That phrase is used sixteen times in the Gospel of John. In every case, it refers to fellowship with Christ.[12] It is not consistent with John's Gospel to suggest this phrase could be applied to a mere *professing* Christian. It always refers to a *true* Christian.

What, then, does the phrase, *in Me* signify? The preposition *in* is used "to designate a close personal relation."[13] One Bible teacher concludes:

> So to abide "in" Christ means to remain in close relationship to Him. What kind of relationship is meant? A review of the 16 occurrences of "in Me" in the Gospel of John seems to suggest that when Jesus used this phrase, He referred to a life of fellowship, a unity of purpose, rather than organic connection.[14]

While Paul sometimes uses the term *in Christ* (not *in Me*) differently in the epistles, to refer to an organic union, John never uses the term in that way to refer to the believer's position in a forensic sense.[15] Rather, John uses the term in the sense of depth of relationship: communion or fellowship.

To abide in Christ, therefore, is to remain in close fellowship with Him, living obediently, loving as He loves, experiencing the closeness as described in John 14:23:

> If a man love me, he will keep my words: and my Father will love
> him, and we will come unto him, and make our abode with him.

What fellowship we can have with Jesus when we choose His pathway of discipleship! The cost of discipleship is great, but the benefits are much greater. Unfortunately, this is not the experience of all believers. Since Jesus commands us to abide in Him, we must conclude it is possible not to abide in Christ. Though all believers are in Him *positionally*, in the Pauline sense, not all Christians are in Him *experientially*, in the Johannine sense. In other words, some believers are fulfilling this command and thereby enjoying sweet communion with Jesus. Other believers are saved from condemnation, but they don't have close fellowship with Jesus. They have union, but not communion. They are missing out on the glorious fellowship for those who are abiding in the vine. They are believers, but have not progressed in discipleship.

Means of Abiding

> As the Father hath loved me, so have I loved you: continue ye in
> my love. If ye keep my commandments, ye shall abide in my love;
> even as I have kept my Father's commandments, and abide in his
> love. John 15:9-10

How do we abide? We remain in Christ by continuing in His love, which is the essence of obeying Him. Of course, the only way we can obey Him is by depending on Him, as we saw in a previous chapter. We trust God to obey Him. So remaining in Christ is continually depending on Him for obedience. The ultimate way obedience is demonstrated in our lives is when we love others as Jesus loves us. That is how discipleship is evidenced.

> A new commandment I give unto you, That ye love one another;
> as I have loved you, that ye also love one another. By this shall all
> men know that ye are my disciples, if ye have love one to another.
> John 13:34-35

One of the common misinterpretations of this text is to suggest it is talking about the saved and the lost. The argument is that those who abide are saved and those who do not abide are demonstrating they never were saved. As we noted, that is incorrect teaching, and here is one reason we know that to be the case. According to vs. 9-10, the way we abide in Christ is by obeying Him. If abiding is a requirement for salvation, then obedience is a requirement for salvation, and that is works-based salvation, the very legalism that Paul condemns in the book of Galatians. We are not saved from hell by obedience! *Not by works of righteousness which we have done, but according to his mercy he saved us,* Titus 3:5.

Are you appropriating the vitality that comes only through the vine? If you are abiding, then you are a disciple indeed. Those who are not abiding will face the severity of Christ's judgment at His Bema Seat.

Results of Abiding

> He that abideth in me, and I in him, the same bringeth forth much fruit: for without me ye can do nothing. Herein is my Father glorified, that ye bear much fruit; so shall ye be my disciples. John 15:5,8

Fruit-Bearing

Those believers who remain with Jesus will bear much fruit. Incidentally, fruit-bearing is not *of* you; it is *through* you. It is *of* the vine; it is of Jesus. You are simply the branch on which the fruit is displayed. You are unable to bear fruit unless you are abiding in the vine, in fellowship with Jesus.

We must remember that the fruit is for the refreshment and nourishment of others, not for the temporal benefit of the branches. That is to say, the fruit is not for you. Andrew Murray writes, "Amid all who surround him he becomes like a tree of life, of which they can taste and be refreshed. He is in his circle a center of life and of blessing, and that simply because he abides in Christ and receives from Him the Spirit of life, of which he can impart to others."[16]

What is the fruit? It is the fruit of the Spirit displayed in your life, the divine characteristics of love, joy, peace, patience, gentleness, goodness, faith, meekness, self-control, etc. It is the fruit of love shown toward others. It is the fruit of compassion for the lost. It is the fruit of our lips giving praise.

It is the fruit of holiness.

> But now being made free from sin, and become servants to God, ye have your fruit unto holiness, and the end everlasting life. Rom. 6:22

> Wherefore, my brethren, ye also are become dead to the law by the body of Christ ... that we should bring forth fruit unto God. For when we were in the flesh, the motions of sins ... did work in our members to bring forth fruit unto death. Rom. 7:4-5

Answered Prayer

Fruit-bearing is the most obvious result of abiding in the vine. But there is another result in the following verses:

> Ye have not chosen me, but I have chosen you, and ordained you, that ye should go and bring forth fruit, and that your fruit should remain: that whatsoever ye shall ask of the Father in my name, he may give it you. John 15:16

> If ye abide in me, and my words abide in you, ye shall ask what ye will, and it shall be done unto you. John 15:7

When you are in close communion with God, you will have the confidence that God is hearing and answering your prayers.

Not Sinning

John gives one additional result of abiding in his first epistle:

> Whosoever abideth in him sinneth not: whosoever sinneth hath not seen him, neither known him. 1 John 3:6

When you are abiding in Him, you are not sinning. Abiding in Christ is living in continuous revival! The problem is that we don't continue in our abiding. Those who are sinning do not have fellowship with Him. It's as if they don't know Him. Keep in mind that John's epistle is not talking about salvation; it's talking about sanctification. It's about communion and fellowship. *If we walk in the light, as He is in the light, we have fellowship one with another,* 1 John 1:7a.

When you are not in fellowship with Jesus because of sin in your life, it is as if you don't know Him; you have become estranged from him. You have union with Him, but not communion. You are not abiding and, consequently, you are not bearing fruit. God is not glorified by your unproductive lifestyle. He is glorified when you, as a believer, choose to count the cost and pay the price of discipleship.

> Herein is my Father glorified, that ye bear much fruit; so shall ye be my disciples. John 15:8

The word *be* at the end of the verse is literally *become*. We become disciples of Jesus by abiding, by remaining with Him, by obeying Him, by loving others, by fellowshipping with Him. Much fruit is the natural outcropping of such a life of discipleship. Sadly, not all believers live like this. Thus, disciples are a subset of believers who have chosen to remain in communion with Jesus.

Consequences of Not Abiding

Jesus says to His disciples, "Keep abiding; stay with Me; continue loving others; remain in communion with me." He says this because He knows our tendency not to continue abiding. The spirit is willing, but the flesh is weak. Just as Peter, who denied Jesus at the cross, got discouraged, and later determined to quit following as a disciple of Christ and go back to his old occupation of fishing, so we have the same tendency. So Jesus admonishes, "Keep on abiding!"

To that end, according to the end of v. 2, the heavenly Father will lovingly purge you and cleanse you so that you will bring forth more fruit. *Every branch that beareth fruit, he purgeth it, that it may bring forth more fruit.* At times, He will nip your buds and prune back your branch through trials and afflictions to help you to grow stronger and healthier, so that you can bear much fruit. Always remember that the vinedresser is loving and patient and kind and merciful. He will always prune you in the way that will benefit you the most as His tender plant. Are you responding rightly to His pruning work in your life?

What about those who choose not to abide? Remember, we're talking about fellowship, not salvation. What will happen if you do not remain in fellowship with God and stop bearing fruit? Though you are eternally secure, God takes the matter of your remaining with Him quite seriously. If you choose not to abide, He has a manner of dealing with His sons, as outlined in Heb. 12. God lovingly disciplines His children, though it may not be obvious to onlookers. Those who continually resist will be dealt with severely at the Judgment Seat.

> Every branch in me that beareth not fruit he taketh away. John 15:2

What does the vinedresser do with non-fruit-bearing branches? The Greek here translated *taketh away* can also mean "lifts up" and several times elsewhere in John's gospel it is used in that sense. Some commentators have suggested that, as a first measure, Jesus carefully lifts up those vines that are not producing, so as to give them an opportunity to produce. In the viticulture of the Middle East, vines will often trail along the ground. The vinedresser has to come along and prop them up so they will become healthy and produce fruit.

God often puts us out of our comfort zone to give opportunities for fellowship with Him. He often customizes trials to prompt us to depend on Him more. He wants our fellowship. To that end, He graciously works with us so we will become fruit-bearing disciples.

What happens to those who continue to resist His working in their lives?

> If a man abide not in me, he is cast forth as a branch, and is withered; and men gather them, and cast them into the fire, and they are burned. John 15:6

Fire in the New Testament does not merely refer to hell. In fact, fire is repeatedly used in the New Testament in reference to the Christian. Heb. 12:29 reminds that *our God is a consuming fire*. That verse is in the context of God's discipline of His children. His discipline is a consuming fire; that is, it consumes the dross in our lives. Furthermore, 1 Cor. 3 warns of the fire at the impending Judgment Seat:

Every man's work shall be made manifest: for the day shall declare
it, because it shall be revealed by fire; and the fire shall try every
man's work of what sort it is. 1 Cor. 3:13

The vine-and-branches passage clearly refers to the saved,
thus the fire is Christ's testing furnace at the Bema. Recognizing that John 15 is a passage for believers on the subject of
discipleship, the context dictates that we view the fire of v. 6,
not as hell-fire, but rather as the Judgment Seat fire. When
branches are persistently not producing, they are cut off and
set aside in a certain area to wither up and later become
burned at the end of the season. So it is with the Christian.

The warning of our Savior is clear. If you are not fellowshipping with Christ, even after His repeated, loving discipline, He will eventually remove you from discipleship
(fellowship), leaving you to your own ways. You will wither
up spiritually, though you remain a child of God. You will
then be put into His testing furnace at the Judgment Seat and
you will be saved, yet so as by fire. Nevertheless, you will be
ashamed as you enter His millennial kingdom with a greatly
diminished capacity for glorifying Him, and you will consciously regret that you did not remain in fellowship with
Christ in this present age. You will probably even shed many
tears. Thus, John the apostle admonishes:

Abide in him; that, when he shall appear, we may have confidence,
and not be ashamed before him at his coming. 1 John 2:28

What about you, dear Christian? If Jesus were to come
right now for His saints, rapturing them up to glory, would
you hang your head in shame because you have not magnified Christ by being a fruit-bearing disciple? Or would you
with confidence lift up your head and smile, knowing you
have pleased the Lord?

---

[12] Robert Dean Jr., "Abiding In Christ: A Dispensational
Theology Of The Spiritual Life (Part 1 Of 3)" *Chafer Theological
Seminary Journal*, Volume 07:1 (Jan 2001), 25-51.

[13]William F. Arndt and F. Wilbur Gingrich, *A Greek-English Lexicon of the New Testament and Other Early Christian Literature* (Chicago: University of Chicago Press, 1957), 259.

[14]Joseph C. Dillow, "Abiding is Remaining in Fellowship," *Bibliotheca Sacra*, 147:585, (Jan 1990), 45-46.

[15] Ibid.

[16]Andrew Murray, *Abide in Christ* (Fort Washington, PA: CLC Publications, 1997), 129-130.

Chapter 5

Suffering Unto Glory

When Stephen preached, the Spirit brought knife-like conviction to his audience, for he was a man filled with the Holy Spirit (see Acts 7). But instead of accepting Stephen's message, the listeners became infuriated and picked up stones to kill him. As he gazed intently into Heaven, Stephen saw the glory of God, and he was able to witness something else, something profound. He saw Jesus, not sitting at the right hand of the Father, but standing. It is likely that Jesus stood because He was moved to action on behalf of Stephen, ready to receive His precious saint with acclamation, ready to pronounce, *Well done*. As Stephen was being pummeled and crushed by the stones, he cried out, *Lord Jesus, receive my spirit*. Stephen surely was received into the presence of Jesus with great joy.

> Blessed is the man that endureth temptation (trials): for when he is tried (approved), he shall receive the crown of life, which the Lord hath promised to them that love him. James 1:12 (paren. added)

In the Scriptures crowns are not merely accolades. They are symbols of rulership to be worn by rulers. Ironically, the Greek word translated *crown* is *stephanos*, which transliterates as *Stephen*, who was the church's first martyr. Undoubtedly, he was richly rewarded for his suffering and will rule with Jesus.

Christ is magnified when you qualify through suffering to become a glorified co-regent with Him in the coming kingdom. To that end, Jesus is leading many sons unto glory.

> 9 But we see Jesus, who was made a little lower than the angels for the suffering of death, crowned with glory and honour; that he by the grace of God should taste death for every man.
> 10 For it became him, for whom are all things, and by whom are all things, in **bringing many sons unto glory**, to make the captain of their salvation perfect through sufferings.
> 11 For both he that sanctifieth and they who are sanctified are all of one: for which cause he is not ashamed to call them brethren,
> 12 Saying, I will declare thy name unto my brethren, in the midst of the church will I sing praise unto thee. Heb. 2:9-12

Jesus is Leading Many Sons to Glory

Who are these sons?

If we were to force a particular theological grid onto this passage, we might tend to conclude these sons are *all* the saints — everyone who has been saved from eternal condemnation. However, that position does not seem to fit this passage. In v. 11 we are told He is not ashamed to call *these* sons brethren, which implies that He is ashamed to call other sons brethren. We will explore this concept later in the chapter, but for now it is important to understand that the Scriptures speak of two classes of saints, not merely one.

> Blessed are the peacemakers: for they shall be called the children of God. Matt. 5:9

This verse is part of the Beatitudes (Matt. 5:3-11), which is part of the greater Sermon on the Mount (Matt. 5-7). The purpose of the Sermon on the Mount is not to teach lost people how to become saved. If it were teaching salvation, it would be propagating works-salvation, and we know that is not the case from the broader context of Scripture. So we must exclude any salvific interpretation. Furthermore, the Sermon on the Mount is not merely outlining the legal system for the coming millennial kingdom. If it were limited to that purpose, it would have little practical application to believers in the present day, and many of the commands would seem non-sensical (for example, see Matt. 5:13-16; 6:19-21).

Jesus preached the Sermon on the Mount for the purpose of instructing saved people how to prepare for the coming kingdom and qualify for rewards in the eternal realm. In other words, Jesus is not focusing on matters of soteriology (salvation), but rather on matters of sanctification and, specifically, preparing to rule in His kingdom.

Teknon vs. Huios

Interestingly, in Matt. 5:9, quoted above, when Jesus refers to *children* of God in this verse, He does not use the Greek word *teknon*, which refers to sons in general (i.e., *children*) but is never used to refer to mature, firstborn sons. Rather, He uses *huios*, the Greek word for mature sons. Notice the following verses with insertions:

> But as many as received him, to them gave he power to become the **sons** (*teknon*) of God, even to them that believe on his name. John 1:12

> Behold, what manner of love the Father hath bestowed upon us, that we should be called the **sons** (*teknon*) of God. 1 John 3:1

Teknon should be translated as *children* in these verses. Contrariwise, in Matt. 5:9 Jesus uses *huios*, which doesn't automatically mean He's referring to firstborn sons who are given an inheritance, but because of the context we can determine it is being used in that way. The same is true later in the chapter.

> But I say unto you, Love your enemies, bless them that curse you, do good to them that hate you, and pray for them which despitefully use you, and persecute you; That ye may be the **children** (*huios*) of your Father which is in heaven: Matt. 5:44-45a

Loving enemies is not how one gets saved, but it *is* how one qualifies to inherit the kingdom. Incidentally, Jesus also used the Greek word *teknon* in the Sermon on the Mount (*children* in Matt. 7:11), so He was clearly distinguishing by His use of terms. The apostle Paul made similar distinctions in Rom. 8.

> The Spirit itself beareth witness with our spirit, that we are the **children** (*teknon*) of God: And if **children** (*teknon*), then heirs; heirs of God. Rom. 8:16-17a

What Paul is saying is that all saints are children of God and, therefore, heirs of God in a general sense. That truth can be corroborated by numerous other New Testament passages of Scripture. However, in the context of this statement Paul is making an obvious contrast between all sons who are heirs of God and a subset of those sons who have gone on to maturity.

> For as many as are led by the Spirit of God, they are the **sons** (*huios*) of God. Rom. 8:14

Again, the *huios* are the sons who are moving on to maturity. So those who are being led of the Spirit — that is, those who are filled with the Spirit, walking in the Spirit (Eph. 5:18; Gal. 5:16) — they are the mature sons of God. The implication is that those who are not walking in the Spirit are not maturing. The distinction in Rom. 8 is vivid. The well-known Greek scholar Henry Alford says, "*Huios* of God differs from *teknon* of God, in implying the higher and more mature and conscious member of God's family."[17]

Adoption of the Firstborn

Furthermore, the *huios* are the ones who have received the spirit of adoption and can cry, *Abba, Father*, a term of endearment.

> For ye have not received the spirit of bondage again to fear; but ye have received the Spirit of adoption, whereby we cry, Abba, Father. Rom. 8:15

It must be remembered that v. 15 follows v. 14, and the context of v. 14 is *huios*, mature sons. Thus, v. 15 must be speaking of mature sons — those that are being led of the Spirit — not all sons in general. It is a sad fact of Christianity that not all saints are being led of the Spirit.

Interestingly, the word *adoption* in the New Testament is *huiothesia* in the Greek. It is based on the root word *huios*. This means that adoption seems to be a unique status conferred on mature, adult sons who receive the inheritance of the first-born. If Paul had intended adoption in this context to refer to all saints, he would surely have used *teknon* as the Greek noun rather than *huios*.

In Bible times, the son designated as firstborn — whether actually first in birth order or not — was given a double por-tion of the Father's inheritance. Firstborn sons by birth could be disqualified from the special inheritance by displeasing the Father (e.g., Jacob conferred the status of firstborn on Joseph rather than Reuben because of Reuben's sinful disqualifica-tion). All sons of God are basic heirs, but only firstborn sons receive special inheritance, reward at the Judgment Seat.

The Glory That Shall Be Revealed

Since we now understand that Paul is making a clear dis-tinction in Rom. 8 between classes of sons, we can compre-hend the point he is making in subsequent verses.

> 17 ... and joint-heirs with Christ; if so be that we suffer with him, that we may be also glorified together.
> 18 For I reckon that the sufferings of this present time are not worthy to be compared with the glory which shall be revealed in us.
> 19 For the earnest expectation of the creature waiteth for the manifestation of the **sons** (*huios*) of God. Rom. 8:17b-19

All children of God are automatically, by nature of our relationship, heirs of God. But all children of God are not, by default, joint-heirs with Christ. We become joint-heirs with Christ only to the extent that we suffer with Him. This is not a given for all saints. It is conditional, reserved only for those who meet the condition. According to the broader context of Rom. 8, the condition is being led of the Spirit, walking in the Spirit (v. 14), and enduring suffering (v. 17). These are the things that qualify a saint as a mature, firstborn son. Look at the glorious result for those who remain as *huios*, mature, firstborn sons. It is found in v. 18 above — glory will be revealed in them. Perhaps another way of saying it is how Paul instructed Timothy:

> If we suffer, we shall also reign with him. 2 Tim. 2:12

Those who endure in their sufferings will be gloriously rewarded. They will be revealed as rulers at the Judgment Seat. Remarkably, all creation is awaiting that glorious day (see Rom. 8:19 above) when the sons (*huios*) of God will be revealed, for the purpose of uniting with Christ in taking back the kingdom of this world from Satan and giving it to Jesus, who alone is worthy. Those whom He deems as *huios* will rule with Him in His kingdom. Indeed, Jesus wants to be the first-born among many brethren (Rom. 8:29) and, to that end, He is preparing many sons unto glory.

The apostle John also used the Greek word *huios* as a distinguishing term.

> He that overcometh shall inherit all things; and I will be his God, and he shall be my **son** (*huios*). Rev. 21:7

This is a promise for overcomers — those who progress in discipleship. They will receive the firstborn reward.

We should not be surprised, then, that the Greek word translated *sons* in our primary text in Heb. 2:10 is *huios,* and it is being used in the same manner — context dictates it. Notice again the primary verse:

> For it became him, for whom are all things, and by whom are all things, in bringing many sons (*huios*) unto glory, to make the captain of their salvation perfect through sufferings. Heb. 2:10

In like manner, as we have seen in the Romans passages above, Heb. 2:10 is not speaking of all saints; it is referring to those whom Jesus is leading to maturity. They are submitted to His progressive sanctification work in their lives, as evidenced in v. 11:

> For both he that sanctifieth and they who are sanctified are all of one: for which cause he is not ashamed to call them brethren, Heb. 2:11

The phrase *they who are sanctified* — because of the tense of the verb in the Greek — should actually read, *those who are being sanctified*. It is not referring to positional sanctification; it's referring to ongoing, progressive (or experiential) sanctification. Robertson says, "It is a process here ... not a single act."[18] Those saints who are being sanctified — set apart unto holiness, conformed to the image of Christ — qualify to become firstborn sons (sons unto glory) if they continue on that path. Unfortunately, not all believers are on that path. They are not cooperating with God, and so they are not being sanctified. Heb. 2:10 does not apply to them. Jesus desires to lead all children of God unto glory, but so few choose to follow Him.

We have answered the question, "Who are these sons?" Now we must consider a second question.

Where is Jesus leading these sons?

The passage says He is leading them *unto glory*, v. 10. Glory only comes from God. In its most literal sense, glory is brightness. Think of Jesus on the Mt. of Transfiguration. Think of Jesus in the eternal state — shining so brightly there is no need of the sun. Glory that is awarded to firstborn sons at the Judgment Seat will result in their shining, to some degree, eternally. We will explore this concept further in Chapter 8.

Most significantly, firstborn sons are being led unto glory for the purpose of reigning.

> For unto the angels hath he not put in subjection the world to come, whereof we speak. Heb. 2:5

If God has not given authority to rule in the coming age to the angels, then to whom has He given it? *Man* will rule the earth, as God originally intended.

> But one in a certain place testified, saying, What is man, that thou art mindful of him? or the son of man, that thou visitest him? Thou madest him a little lower than the angels; thou crownedst him with glory and honour, and didst set him over the works of thy hands: Thou hast put all things in subjection under his feet ... But now we see not yet all things put under him. Heb. 2:6-8

The writer quotes Psalm 8 and refers back to the original position of man at creation. God made man to rule the earth and put everything in subjection to Adam. *But now we see not yet all things put under him.* What happened? Adam sinned and thereby forfeited his dominion over the earth to Satan. That was not God's original intent. Ah, but God had a plan from eternity past, before the foundation of the world:

> But we see Jesus, who was made a little lower than the angels for the suffering of death, crowned with glory and honour. Heb. 2:9

> For he must reign, till he hath put all enemies under his feet. 1 Cor. 15:25

Jesus came and was born of a woman; He took on human flesh *for the suffering of death.* He was born to die on Calvary and pay the price for our sins. He thereby defeated Satan through His death and resurrection (Heb. 2:14). For His obedience and suffering, He was given the distinction of firstborn Son and *crowned with glory and honor.* Angels will not rule over the coming millennial Earth, because Jesus will! But He does not desire to rule by Himself. Another glorious aspect of the Father's plan from before the foundation of the world is that Jesus will bring with Him into His ruling realm many sons unto glory. Jesus will share His authority with co-regents — mature, firstborn sons whom He ordains to rule with Him. That has been His intent and purpose all along, even from before the foundation of the world.

> Do ye not know that the saints shall judge the world? 1 Cor. 6:2

> Know ye not that we shall judge angels? 1 Cor. 6:3

Perhaps one of the reasons Christ has not yet returned is not only so that people from every kindred and tongue and people and nation can be saved and thus surround His throne one day, but also so that many sons can be brought unto glory to rule with Him in righteousness.

We have answered two critical questions that arise from a study of Heb. 2:10. First, who are the sons that Jesus is leading to glory? Second, where is He leading them? We now come to a third question. How is Jesus leading the sons unto glory?

What is the means by which they are being led? This is the most painful part of the truth, and we have already hinted at the answer earlier in this chapter.

Sons are Made Perfect Through Suffering

To make the captain of their salvation perfect through sufferings. Four key words need to be defined in our text. First, the *salvation* mentioned in v. 10 is the salvation of one's soul at the Judgment Seat, not initial salvation of one's spirit from eternal condemnation. It is *future* salvation, not *past* salvation. It is persevering in sanctification unto reward. (For a fuller explanation, see Chapter 3, "The Paradox of Saving the Soul," in my previous book, *The End of the Pilgrimage.*). In fact, the use of the word *salvation* in the book of Hebrews is always with respect to soul-salvation (1:14; 2:3; 2:10; 5:9; 6:9; 9:28).

Second, to make *perfect* does not mean one becomes sinless. Perfection in the New Testament means to reach the goal of sanctification, which is conformity to Christ. The Greek word for *perfect* means to complete or accomplish — to reach the goal — and it is akin to the Greek word used by Jesus when He said on the cross, *It is finished,* John 19:30. By that He meant, "My task has been fulfilled; I have completed the will of the Father." In the sense of progressive sanctification, it is the idea of a believer going all the way in discipleship so that he receives a positive verdict at the Judgment Seat.

Third, the word *captain* is the idea of one who is over others. It could translate as *chief* or even *prince.* So the Prince of our salvation is not merely referring to Jesus who died for the sins of mankind to rescue us from damnation. In this context, it is referring to Jesus who is leading sons to glory, through the painful means of suffering, so that He might be the first-born among many (firstborn) brethren.

Fourth, it is therefore imperative to understand the word *sufferings* and, in particular, how it relates to being perfected.

Though he were a Son, yet learned he obedience by the things which he suffered; And being made perfect, he became the author of eternal salvation unto all them that obey him. Heb. 5:9

The Nature of Suffering

Jesus learned obedience through suffering. This does not mean He had previously sinned and then learned to stop sinning by suffering. God forbid! Jesus was without sin. What it means is that He learned full compliance and submission to the Father's will — *as a man* — through the means of suffering. As a result, Jesus became the author of eternal salvation — that is, soul-salvation or reward at the Judgment Seat. He is now the *captain* of soul-salvation for those who learn obedience in their sufferings.

Remarkably, just as Jesus learned obedience through suffering, so do we, to the extent we are yielded to the process. Having been perfected in His sufferings, Jesus is now working to perfect submissive saints, with the intent of leading those to glory who will follow His example of endurance in suffering.

Obedience in sufferings is not merely experiencing troubles and hardships. All saints will face hardships throughout life. That, of itself, is no guarantee one is being perfected. Rather, becoming perfected in sufferings is the idea of consistently enduring sufferings in a spirit of Christlikeness. The hymn, *O to Be Like Thee!* captures the thought beautifully in the phrase, "meekly enduring cruel reproaches, willing to suffer others to save."[19] The writer to the Hebrews seeks to motivate saints to endure suffering by focusing attention on Jesus, the consummate example:

> Wherefore seeing we also are compassed about with so great a cloud of witnesses, let us lay aside every weight, and the sin which doth so easily beset us, and let us run with patience the race that is set before us, Looking unto Jesus the author and finisher of our faith; who for the joy that was set before him endured the cross, despising the shame, and is set down at the right hand of the throne of God. For consider him that endured such contradiction of sinners against himself, lest ye be wearied and faint in your minds. Heb. 12:1-3

Who for the joy that was set before Him endured the cross. What was the joy set before Him? The joy wasn't the cross and bearing the sins of the whole world. The joy before Him was the *hope* of reclaiming the kingdom and regaining rule of Earth as the second Adam. The joy before Him was (and is) bringing many sons to glory. Consider the parable of the talents in Matt. 25:14-30. In the end of the passage, when the servants are called upon to give an accounting to the Master, the faithful ones hear these precious words:

> Well done, good and faithful servant; thou hast been faithful over a few things, I will make thee ruler over many things: enter thou into the joy of thy lord. Matt. 25:23

Christ's joy can become our joy too — the prospect of becoming sons unto glory — if we endure our sufferings in like manner as He endured His sufferings. That is why we are to count it all joy when we face various trials (James 1:2). That is why we are told to look to Jesus as we are running the race (Heb. 12:1-3). That is why we are told to consider Him that endured the cross and then sat down at the right hand of God as victor. We can also endure our sufferings with His enablement and then sit down next to Him on an actual throne in the world to come.

We are told in Heb. 12:3 to consider Jesus enduring His sufferings so we don't get weary amidst our sufferings. Then the writer to the Hebrews continues into a discussion about God's chastening in the lives of His children (Heb. 12:4-11). We are instructed to endure chastening, knowing He is producing in us *the peaceable fruit of righteousness*, Heb. 12:11.

Suffering is critically important. Incidentally, it is not limited to persecution. That's only one type of suffering. Other types of suffering include: denying self, graciously accepting deprivations, and enduring trials and temptations in the spirit of Christ. When you suffer in this manner you will grow in grace, become perfected in sanctification, and identify with Jesus in His sufferings. There is something quite beautiful about it. The heart cry of the apostle Paul sums it up well.

> I count all things but loss for the excellency of the knowledge of Christ Jesus my Lord: for whom I have suffered the loss of all things, and do count them but dung, that I may win Christ, and be found in him ... That I may know him, and the power of his resurrection, and **the fellowship of his sufferings**, being made conformable unto his death; If by any means I might attain unto

the resurrection of the dead. I press toward the mark for the prize of the high calling of God in Christ Jesus. Phil. 3:8-11, 14

Fellowship in — or participation in — Christ's sufferings is the means by which you can obtain the prize of the high calling. When you submit with a spirit of Christlikeness in suffering, you will learn obedience and draw closer in fellowship to Him. In other words, suffering perfects the saint into a mature son — you are made perfect through suffering. Only on this pathway will you become qualified for *the prize of the high calling.* The benefits are incredibly glorious.

Benefit #1: Oneness With Christ

For both he that sanctifieth and they who are sanctified are all of one, Heb. 2:11a. Jesus, who does the sanctifying work of setting apart and making holy, becomes one with those who are submitting to His sanctifying work. Simply put, when you endure sufferings as Christ, you become *one* with Christ.

> And the glory which thou gavest me I have given them; that they may be one, even as we are one: I in them, and thou in me, that they may be made perfect in one; and that the world may know that thou hast sent me, and hast loved them, as thou hast loved me. John 17:22-23

What an incredible prospect! Do you see the importance of identifying with Christ in His sufferings by enduring yours?

Benefit #2: Exaltation Before the Brethren

For which cause he is not ashamed to call them brethren, Heb. 2:11b. For those who are being sanctified, being made perfect by enduring their sufferings, Jesus is not ashamed to call them brethren. We know that He *is* ashamed to use the endearing term *brethren* to refer to unfaithful children of God.

> For whosoever shall be ashamed of me and of my words, of him shall the Son of man be ashamed, when he shall come in his own glory, and in his Father's, and of the holy angels. Luke 9:26 (see also Mark 8:38)

In the context of Luke 9:26, Jesus is speaking to saved people about the need to progress in discipleship. Those who do not cooperate with God in their Christian walk, choosing instead the path of carnal, fleshly living, will be ashamed of Christ and His Word in this world, and He will be ashamed of them at His judgment bar. However, Jesus is not ashamed of those brethren who are submitting to discipleship and enduring suffering and thereby being led unto glory. They are His firstborn sons who are worthy of special inheritance, the subset deemed worthy of reward and ruling with Jesus. The apostle Paul also wrote about this truth.

> 10 Therefore I endure all things for the elect's sakes, that they may also obtain the salvation which is in Christ Jesus with eternal glory.
> 11 It is a faithful saying: For if we be dead with him, we shall also live with him:
> 12 If we suffer, we shall also reign with him: if we deny him, he also will deny us:
> 13 If we believe not, yet he abideth faithful: he cannot deny himself. 2 Timothy 2:10-13

Paul is saying that he is willing to endure any kind of suffering or hardship so that other saints, by his example, might also be led to obtain *the salvation ... with eternal glory.* Paul is not speaking of initial salvation from eternal condemnation. As in the book of Hebrews, so the apostle here is referring to soul-salvation, or reward at the Judgment Seat, which is reserved only for those who endure in faithfulness.

Paul's point in v. 11 is that all saints died with Christ and rose with Christ (Rom. 6:4); that is their positional, legal standing. And so Paul can emphatically say in v. 13 that even if a saint does not live in daily dependence on Christ, that saint is still saved, for Christ cannot deny His Word. In 1 Cor. 3:15 he puts it another way, saying that saints of this nature are *saved, yet so as by fire.* However, in v. 12 Paul makes the same point that Christ had made. He warns those saints who are not living the Christ-life of victory, who are not enduring in suffering, that Jesus will deny them the privilege of ruling in His kingdom. Only those who are enduring will reign with Him.

Undoubtedly, this is the same truth being shared in the

book of Hebrews. In fact, the writer to the Hebrews goes one step further. *I will declare thy name unto my brethren, in the midst of the church will I sing praise unto thee*, Heb. 2:12. Not only does Jesus refer to sons of glory as *brethren*, He also exults in these faithful ones; He is proud of them and declares them as His own. In other words, there is an amazing camaraderie among the firstborn. They are one, for they are spiritually on the same page, and they are publicized as cohorts of Christ. Again, this is a special privilege only for those saints that qualify.

Imagine a saint being singled out by Jesus at His Judgment Seat and hearing, *Well done, good and faithful servant. Thou hast been faithful over a few things; I will make thee ruler over many things*. Then hear Him declaring before all the saints, "Brethren, I want you to meet one of my sons of glory — this one will rule with me in my kingdom!" On the other hand, imagine Jesus confronting a child of God who has been disobedient and who has chafed at suffering or lashed back at persecutors. Perhaps Christ will say, "Thou wicked and slothful servant; I am ashamed of you and cannot confess you before the Father or before the brethren as one of my sons of glory." Visualize the weeping and sorrow and shame over such a verdict. This is a matter of utmost seriousness.

Jesus is Made Perfect By Leading Sons to Glory

The above heading may sound odd, especially since — according to Heb. 5:9 — Jesus has already been made perfect. Nevertheless, Heb. 2:10 says, *It became Him*, it was fitting, that in leading many sons to glory, those sons — through their sufferings — would make perfect the Prince of their salvation. What does this mean?

Keep in mind that *to make perfect* is to bring to completion. How is Jesus brought to completion by leading sons to glory? In the marvelous plan of God, as Christ's past sufferings are connected with our present sufferings, and thereby many sons are led to glory, the ultimate goal of Christ's suffering and death is reached: The kingdom of Earth will be reclaimed by King Jesus, and He has co-regents who will reign with Him eternally. In that sense, He is made perfect — He is brought to completion — when sons are brought to glory. Magnificent!

Peter says something similar in his first epistle.

> That the trial of your faith, being much more precious than of gold that perisheth, though it be tried with fire, might be found unto praise and honour and glory at the appearing of Jesus Christ: Whom having not seen, ye love; in whom, though now ye see him not, yet believing, ye rejoice with joy unspeakable and full of glory: Receiving the end of your faith, even the salvation of your souls. Of which salvation the prophets have enquired and searched diligently, who prophesied of the grace that should come unto you: Searching what, or what manner of time the Spirit of Christ which was in them did signify, when it testified beforehand the sufferings of Christ, and the glory that should follow. 1 Pet. 1:7-11

When the sufferings of Christ become our sufferings — that is, when we fellowship (participate) in His sufferings and become conformable to His death — we enter into His joy, the joy of future co-ruling. The prophets of the Old Testament were perplexed, not so much by the sufferings of Christ, but with the future glory thereafter. They got only a glimpse of it, but apparently could not figure out how it would come to be. But we know because the book of Hebrews tells us. He is bringing many sons unto glory.

Before the fall, when Adam needed a co-regent, a bride, God opened up Adam's side and took a rib to make a completer for him. Adam referred to Eve as *bone of my bones, and flesh of my flesh,* Gen. 2:23. Together, they were complete. Without Eve, Adam was incomplete. Jesus, the second Adam, has a body too, known as the church, those who have been redeemed by His blood. In fulfillment of the type, Christ's bride will be taken from His body, as Adam's bride was taken from his body. That bride is comprised of many sons brought unto glory. When that bride is presented to Him after the Judgment Seat, Christ will be complete, ready to rule as Adam was ready to rule. *That* is what Heb. 2:10 means.

Do you want to be one of those sons led to glory that comprises His bride? Then you must choose to enter into His sufferings by enduring your sufferings by His grace — doing so out of the joy that is set before you. You cannot do this of yourself. The earlier chapters of this book describe the provision whereby you can live in obedience and victory, even in the midst of great pressure and even intense suffering.

He that overcometh shall inherit all things; and I will be his God, and he shall be my son. Rev. 21:7

For further study on this important subject, see 1 Pet. 4:12-19, 2 Thess. 1:3-12 and Matt. 5:10-12.

---

[17] Henry Alford, "Romans," in *Alford's Greek Testament: An Exegetical and Critical Commentary* (Bellingham, WA: Logos Bible Software, 2010), 2:391.

[18] A. T. Robertson, *Word Pictures in the New Testament* (Grand Rapids, MI: Baker Book House, 1960), vol. 5, 348.

[19] Thomas O. Chisholm, "O to Be Like Thee!" (No. 316) in *Great Hymns of the Faith.*

Chapter 6

Developing an
Eternal Worldview

Have you heard about the treasure of Forrest Fenn? It is a bronze chest filled with jewelry, figurines, precious gems, and piles of gold coins and nuggets — the kind of loot you might expect to find in a pirate's treasure chest. Mr. Fenn hid the chest somewhere in the Rocky Mountains, and he offers it as a prize, "with no strings attached," to whoever finds it. Are you ready to go treasure hunting? Let me first tell you the back-story.

Mr. Fenn, an elderly multimillionaire businessman and decorated Vietnam veteran from Santa Fe, New Mexico, decided after receiving a cancer prognosis to pass along some of his wealth to mankind in a unique way. He packed the treasure chest full of the highly valuable items and concealed its whereabouts in the year 2010. Then he wrote a poem in his autobiography, giving numerous clues to help seekers find the treasure box. As of the writing of this book, the treasure remains undiscovered, despite an estimated crowd of thirty thousand treasure seekers having searched for it since it was hidden.[20]

That is quite a story, and a true one. Let's talk about those treasure hunters for a moment. They are obviously driven by several considerations. **First,** they believe there is, indeed, hidden treasure. **Second,** they are convinced it can be found. **Third,** they individually expect they will be the one to find it. **Fourth,** they willingly expend an enormous amount of time and resources hunting for it. **Fifth,** they search eagerly — with great diligence, perhaps even night and day — to obtain their potential reward. We might even suggest the treasure seekers are obsessed with finding the treasure.

Spiritual Treasure Seekers

God expects the same intensity from *spiritual* treasure seekers, when He uses the word *seek* in the following verses:

> 1 If ye then be risen with Christ, **seek** those things which are above, where Christ sitteth on the right hand of God.
> 2 Set your affection on things above, not on things on the earth.
> 3 For ye are dead, and your life is hid with Christ in God.
> 4 When Christ, who is our life, shall appear, then shall ye also appear with him in glory. Col. 3:1-4

> But **seek** ye first the kingdom of God, and his righteousness; and all these things shall be added unto you. Matt. 6:33

Intensity is implied in the word *seek*. God wants His children to believe there is actually a special treasure we can obtain, and He wants us to pursue it. Furthermore, He knows it will require an enormous amount of time and resources on our part as we seek the things that are above. Nonetheless, He wants us to strive for it — seeking eagerly, with great diligence — that we might inherit our reward.

Unfortunately, not all of God's children expend the effort. Some don't see the significance of seeking things that are above; they don't believe there is a treasure to be found. Others believe they already possess it by default of their salvation. They are, of course, mistaken. Perhaps others know there is treasure to be found, but they are unwilling to pay the price to obtain it. Are you willing to seek those things that are above? The reward is beyond comprehension. In one word, at the end of v. 4, it is called *glory*. We might say it is *glorious*.

We are to seek things that are *above* — things that are otherworldly — things of the heavenly realm.

> And he said unto them, Ye are from beneath; I am from above: ye are of this world; I am not of this world. John 8:23

An Eternal Worldview

So we are to seek the things of His world, the world from whence He came, things that are above. God wants us to develop an eternal worldview. Someone may wonder, "Don't all Christians already possess an eternal worldview?" If all Christians possess an eternal worldview by default, then God would not need to remind us, *Seek those things that are above.* Sadly, very few Christians truly have an *eternal* worldview. What we all should have, by default of our salvation, is a *Christian* worldview. Incidentally, by *worldview* I mean the framework by which you interpret life and the world, your philosophy of life.

Everyone has a worldview, of course. You may not be able to articulate it, but you have one. As a Christian, you believe in God and Satan and Heaven and Hell and angels, even though you can't see those beings or those places. You believe God created the heaven and the earth. You believe in morality and absolute truth as taught in the Word of God. You believe Jesus is fully God and fully man. You believe He left Heaven's glories, became virgin born, lived a sinless life, and willingly submitted to be crucified. You believe He rose again and that today He is seated at the right hand of the Father. You believe you should share this message with other people. Because of those beliefs you interpret life and the world through that lens. It is your philosophy of life, your way of viewing things, and it drives your thinking and your assessment of all that happens in this world. It is your Christian (some may call it *biblical*) worldview.

All Christians *should* have a Christian worldview. But that is not what Paul is calling us to in Col. 3. He assumes you already believe these things and you, therefore, view life through a Christian perspective. Based on that foundation, the apostle is calling us to something greater, something higher, something we could call an eternal worldview.

Christ is magnified when you adopt an eternal world-view, a heavenly way of thinking. Lightfoot says, "You must not only *seek* heaven; you must also *think* heaven."[21] How does one develop an *eternal* worldview?

Perceiving Eternal Realities

All Christians should believe in God and Satan, angelic beings, Heaven and Hell, and so on. Those are the planks of a Christian worldview platform, as described earlier. *Perceiving* eternal realities, however, is more than merely believing in the existence of eternal things. Perceiving eternal realities is seeing the *interaction* of the eternal realm with your daily life in a human body on Earth. So often, even as Christians, we go along in life believing in eternal things, but we don't perceive eternal realities at work — everyday — in our lives. Rather, we tend to forget about the eternal world, believing it doctrinally, but not interacting with it practically. One who has an eternal worldview *never* forgets about the spirit realm. It is continually on their mind, for they live as if it were real and interactive.

A classic illustration of this point can be found in 2 Kings 6. By way of background, the King of Syria is waging warfare against Israel. Elisha the prophet is given revelation by God as to the enemy's position, and he conveys this intelligence to the King of Israel, who is spared being attacked on numerous occasions because of it. The King of Syria gets quite upset about this and — hearing from his generals that Elisha is the one giving away their position — sends horses, chariots, and a massive army to surround the city of Dothan where Elisha dwells.

> Therefore sent he thither horses, and chariots, and a great host: and they came by night, and compassed the city about. And when the servant of the man of God was risen early, and gone forth, behold, an host compassed the city both with horses and chariots. And his servant said unto him, Alas, my master! how shall we do?
> 2 Kings 6:14-15

The response of Elisha's servant represents the response of the typical Christian who may have a Christian worldview but not an eternal worldview. *Alas, how shall we do?* In modern colloquial it would translate, "Oh no! We're doomed!" The tendency is to look upon the temporal crisis at hand and panic or get anxious or angry, rather than see the provision of God in the eternal realm. Elisha, on the other hand, views things quite differently.

> And he answered, Fear not: for they that be with us are more than they that be with them. 2 Kings 6:16

Elisha sees more than just the problem at hand. He doesn't merely believe in the eternal realm. He sees the eternal realm and interacts with it.

> And Elisha prayed, and said, LORD, I pray thee, open his eyes, that he may see. And the LORD opened the eyes of the young man; and he saw: and, behold, the mountain was full of horses and chariots of fire round about Elisha. 2 Kings 6:17

After Elisha prays, the servant sees. His perspective is broadened so that he not only believes in the spirit realm, he now perceives those realities and sees their interaction in his life, as Elisha does. The eternal realm can be just as real to us, not through physical eyes, but through eyes of faith. While perception of *physical* realities is through the senses, perception of *eternal* realities is through faith. *For we walk by faith, not by sight,* 2 Cor. 5:7. Incidentally, this is typically not something one comprehends instantly. It is learned, over time, as God teaches us the realities of the eternal realm and how it intersects with our physical life.

We need to stop living as Elisha's servant, who was certainly aware of the spirit realm (how could he *not* be as Elisha's servant?), yet he was not seeing the interface between that realm and this. But when Elisha prayed — when Elisha interacted with the spirit realm, asking for his servant's eyes to be opened — the servant came to understand realities that he had never grasped previously. We need to see the same through eyes of faith, not merely believing in the reality of Heaven and Hell and God and Satan, but perceiving how all of that relates to everyday life.

Believing Eternal Verities

Verities are truths of critical importance. *Eternal* verities are truths of critical importance that transcend *earthly* verities. Eternal verities are Bible truths about the eternal realm and our interaction with that realm. Putting it another way, eternal verities are the *modus operandi* of Heaven, a Latin term meaning the mode of operation, or the way something functions or operates. The modus operandi of the heavenly realm is entirely different than the modus operandi of the earthly realm. The way Heaven operates is different than the way Earth operates. Heaven's way of doing business is God's way, not man's way.

God says, "I will supply all your need." Man says, "I have to supply my own need." God says, "Nothing can separate you from God's love." Man says, "Bad things in my life make me feel as if God doesn't love me." God says, "You can do all things through Christ who strengthens you." Man says, "*I* can do this." God says, "Put on the whole armor of God so you may be able to stand against the wiles of the devil." Man says, "What's the use; the armor doesn't help; I've tried it and failed," or worse yet, "I can withstand temptation." God says, "Whatever you ask in prayer, believing, you will receive." Man says, "My prayer wasn't answered." God says, "If you confess your sin, I am faithful and just to forgive you of your sin and cleanse you." Man says, "I still feel guilty."

The point is eternal verities are not naturally accepted by saints. Do you see that? Our flesh is predisposed to oppose God's modus operandi. Only those who truly believe eternal verities have an eternal worldview; all others have an earthly worldview. Here's an illustration. God says, "All things work together for good to them that love God." Virtually all saints would say they believe that, but only some really believe as if it were the case. When troubling things come along in life, do you recognize that God — who is of the eternal realm — is using difficult people and circumstances in the earthly realm to make you better? If so, you will trust God completely amidst your overwhelming trials. Other believers don't seem to accept their trials as of the Lord, intended to make them better. So they chafe at trials and tribulations and complain and do everything in their power to try to escape the pressures. Does that describe you? If so, your wrong response of fear, discouragement, worry, or whatever, betrays your statement of belief that all things work together for good. It does no good to *say* you believe eternal verities such as Rom. 8:28 if, in reality, you don't *act* as if you believe them. That's really the point James is making in chapter two of his epistle. You can talk all you want about your faith in the Lord as a believer, but "where the rubber meets the road" is your actual response when the going gets tough. Do you believe eternal verities? Do you evidence your belief by your responses and actions?

Why is it that you struggle with eternal verities? It is because you really do not believe; you require sight. The world system dictates against believing in the eternal realm because it cannot be seen. It insists that *seeing is believing*. God, on the contrary, says that *believing is seeing*.

> Then said Jesus unto him, Except ye see signs and wonders, ye will not believe. John 4:48

> Jesus answered and said unto them, This is the work of God, that ye believe on him whom he hath sent. They said therefore unto him, What sign shewest thou then, that we may see, and believe thee? what dost thou work? But I said unto you, That ye also have seen me, and believe not. John 6:29-30, 36

> Jesus saith unto her, Said I not unto thee, that, if thou wouldest believe, thou shouldest see the glory of God? John 11:40

> Jesus saith unto him, Thomas, because thou hast seen me, thou hast believed: blessed are they that have not seen, and yet have believed. John 20:29

Man says one must see in order to believe; God says one must believe in order to see. What a radical difference! Those who have an eternal worldview do things in God's order. They believe first and then are enabled by God to see.

Embracing Eternal Values

Set your affection on things above, not on things on the earth. God has to command this because our natural tendency is to have affection for earthly things. He wants us to have heavenly, eternal values. Your values are what you hold dear — those things you consider to have worth or importance in your life. The things you value are the things you love, the things you really care about. Jesus said, "Where your treasure is, there will your heart be also." Your heart follows what it holds dear.

What we tend to hold dear is not what God holds dear. His values and our values are often not synchronized. Consider Jesus: Though He lived on Earth, His values were entirely heavenly. He said to His disciples, *My meat is to do the will of Him that sent me, and to finish His work,* John 4:34. Jesus was consumed with the Father's will. Indeed, He cried out in prayer to the Father, *Not my will, but thine, be done,* Luke 22:42. In the Lord's prayer He asked, *Thy kingdom come. Thy will be done in earth, as it is in heaven,* Matt. 6:10. He embraced eternal values, and He asks the same of us.

Multitudes of saints have set their affection on things on the earth, temporal things — money, possessions, prestige, even relationships. If we are to set our affection on things above, then we must disavow earthly values. Perhaps you are driven by money and possessions. God wants you to be willing to give up everything and be content in Him. Maybe you enjoy your comforts. God wants you to be willing to endure anything for His sake. Could it be your agenda is driving your life? God wants it to be *His* agenda. If you are attached to *your* music or *your* fashions or *your* media or *your* entertainment or *your* possessions, then you do not have eternal values. When you, dear saint of God, "Turn your eyes upon Jesus, look full in His wonderful face, and the things of earth will grow strangely dim in the light of His glory and grace."[22]

A Personal Testimony

I will never forget when God first began teaching me about the eternal realm. When I was in my mid-twenties, I was focused on making money in the business world. My college degree was in finance, the Lord had given me a solid corporate position in a major Chicago corporation, and I was just starting to experience some success toward my personal goals. I was a Christian and had a solid Christian worldview. I was active in my local church and living a decent Christian life. But, unfortunately, my values were wrong. I was not setting my affection on things above, but rather on things of Earth.

Thankfully, God arrested my attention with a verse of Scripture — a verse that seemed to "pop off" the page when I read it one morning while having my devotions. It has since become my life verse:

> While we look not at the things which are seen, but at the things which are not seen: for the things which are seen are temporal; but the things which are not seen are eternal. 2 Cor. 4:18

Little did I know this verse of Scripture would radically change my life. However, I dismissed it as nothing significant at the time and went on with my temporal values. Then my pastor preached a message on that same verse shortly thereafter. The Lord grabbed my attention once again, but I foolishly dismissed it as not relevant to my life situation. The last straw was when I heard the verse quoted on Moody radio on my way to work one day. Then it struck me: My values are earthly and temporal, not heavenly and eternal. I confessed my sinful attitude to the Lord and yielded my heart to Him. That was only the first step in what has become an ongoing pilgrimage toward an eternal worldview. Shortly after submitting my values to the Lord, He called me to pastoral ministry. I am so thankful for the Lord's patience and continued working in my life.

I Have Decided to Follow Jesus

Many do not know the story behind the words of the well-known chorus, *I Have Decided to Follow Jesus*. In the nineteenth century a Welsh missionary traveled to Assam in northeast India to give the gospel to the tribal peoples of that region. One of the first he saw converted to Christ was an Indian man, along with the man's wife and children. The newly-saved man was persecuted by the people of his village, and the day came when his faith was put to the ultimate test. The village chief called upon the man to renounce his faith in Christ or be put to death. The man said, "I have decided to follow Jesus; no turning back." The chief ordered the execution of the man's wife and children before his eyes. They were instantly massacred by a shower of arrows. Tearfully but confidently, the Christian man responded, "Though no one join me, still I will follow; no turning back." Furious, the chief demanded that the convert recant immediately or die. Without hesitation, the man said, "The world behind me, the cross before me; no turning back." The man was brutally put to death, but his Christlike response reportedly led to the conversion of many in that village.

When a child of God has an eternal worldview, nothing else matters in life.

---

[20] "Fenn Treasure," *Wikipedia: The Free Encyclopedia* (accessed Dec., 2015).

[21] J. B. Lightfoot, *St. Paul's Epistles to the Colossians and Philemon* (Peabody, MA: Hendrickson Publ., 1995), 209.

[22] Helen H. Lemmel, "Turn Your Eyes Upon Jesus" (No. 204) in *Great Hymns of the Faith*.

Chapter 7

Appropriating Heavenly Power

Incredible power is at the disposal of every saint. So few choose to appropriate — take possession — of the power that our omnipotent God makes readily available to His children. It could be some are unaware of the power. Incidentally, the power belongs to God, not to us; we have no inherent power of our own. Nevertheless, He graciously offers it to us, and if we would properly prepare to inherit His coming kingdom, then we must draw upon His power throughout our Christian walk. For as the apostle Paul said, *The kingdom of God is not in word, but in power*, 1 Cor. 4:20. It is important, therefore, that saints learn to live and minister in the power of God, taking possession of it here and now. Those who are developing an eternal worldview will be appropriating the power proffered by God. The apostle Paul prayed that believers at Ephesus would know the exceeding greatness of God's power — the very power that led to Christ's resurrection and exaltation and will lead to ours too, if we will draw upon it.

That ye may know what is the hope of his calling, and what the riches of the glory of his inheritance in the saints, and what is the exceeding greatness of his power to us-ward who believe, according to the working of his mighty power, which he wrought in Christ, when he raised him from the dead, and set him at his own right hand in the heavenly places, far above all principality, and power, and might, and dominion, and every name that is named, not only in this world, but also in that which is to come: Eph. 1:18-21

Christ is magnified when you draw upon His divine power for conquering the enemy and for ministering effectively.

God offers to His children different types of power, and each one is critical to understand and utilize when needed. By not making use of the particular power that has been provided, you will experience defeat and failure on every occasion. It is, therefore, imperative to avail yourself of God's appointed provision.

Power over Sin

In Chapter 2, *Reckoning the Paradoxes*, we spoke to the wonderful truth that sin is powerless to rule the child of God, and the importance of reckoning that fact in order to walk in victory. But in that chapter we stopped short of discussing one of the applications for everyday living.

Clarifying Positional vs. Practical Sanctification

All children of God have been justified and, therefore, stand positionally righteous and sanctified (set apart) before God. That transaction occurred at the point of salvation of our spirit from eternal condemnation. It is part of God's gift. Peter emphasizes the positional aspect of sanctification in his second epistle:

According as his divine power hath given unto us all things that pertain unto life and godliness, through the knowledge of him that hath called us to glory and virtue. 2 Pet. 1:3

As a result, you have everything you need to live a life of victory over sin. It is your provision and was given to you when you trusted Christ for eternal life and consequently died with Him and rose with Him (Rom. 6; Gal. 2:20).

Nevertheless, the power of that transaction is of no benefit unless appropriated. As stated earlier, we appropriate our provision — that is, His grace — by faith (Rom. 5:2). When we depend on the Holy Spirit who lives within to obey God, we experience God's sanctifying work in our everyday lives. The righteousness of God's law is fulfilled in our lives to the extent we walk in the Spirit and not according to the flesh (Rom. 8:4). That is called *progressive* or *experiential* sanctification. It is based upon *positional* sanctification, but it does not progress unconditionally. *Progressive* sanctification requires appropriation by faith. Peter also speaks to this practical side of sanctification.

> Whereby are given unto us exceeding great and precious promises: that by these ye might be partakers of the divine nature, having escaped the corruption that is in the world through lust.
> 2 Pet. 1:4

By claiming God's promises — or, putting it differently, by depending on God's enabling grace — we become experiential participants in Christ's divine nature and escape the corrupting influence of the world. Paul uses very practical terminology to help us understand how this plays out in everyday living.

Put Off and Put On

Notice the words and phrases emphasized in the following Scripture passage:

> 5 Mortify therefore your members which are upon the earth; fornication, uncleanness, inordinate affection, evil concupiscence, and covetousness, which is idolatry:
> 8 **Put off** all these; anger, wrath, malice, blasphemy, filthy communication out of your mouth.
> 9 Lie not one to another, seeing that **ye have put off the old man** with his deeds;
> 10 **And have put on the new man**, which is renewed in knowledge after the image of him that created him:
> 12 **Put on** therefore, as the elect of God, holy and beloved, bowels of mercies, kindness, humbleness of mind, meekness, long-suffering;

13 Forbearing one another, and forgiving one another, if any man have a quarrel against any: even as Christ forgave you, so also do ye.
14 And above all these things put on charity, which is the bond of perfectness. Col. 3:5, 8-10, 12-14

In v. 8 Paul commands that works of the flesh be *put off* and in v. 12 that graces of the Christian life be *put on.* If we were to stop there, we might tend to think this is to be done solely of our own effort. What is the key to putting off and putting on? It is understanding that you *already have put off* the old man and *have put on* the new man. Of course, as we learned in Chapter 2, that happened at the point of initial salvation. A divine transaction occurred when you died with Christ and rose with Him. Positionally, you have already put off the old and put on the new. Indeed, God did that work in your *spirit.* What that means is that your *soul* now has the opportunity to draw upon the provision that resides in your *spirit* and thereby to put off sin and put on spiritual graces in your Christian life. Because of the indwelling Holy Spirit, you have the power, as v. 5 commands, to *mortify* — to put to death — sins of the flesh.

On the flip side, it is also possible for you to put on the things mentioned in vs. 12-14 — mercy, kindness, humility, meekness, longsuffering, forbearance, forgiveness, and love. You really can put on those things because, as v. 10 says, your new man has already been put on. Those who are seeking to magnify Christ will be regularly appropriating power for adding these virtues. It is important to admit that, of yourself, you are completely incapable of doing this. Our prideful human nature thinks we can do it, and so we try really hard. But inevitably there is failure because our trying is driven by self-effort. Anything we do on our own is repulsive in the nostrils of God because it is not accomplished in partnership with Him.

The graces listed in vs. 12ff can only be produced by the Holy Spirit as we depend upon Him, and the sins mentioned in vs. 5ff can only be forsaken by obedience to and dependence on the Holy Spirit. Paul sums it up beautifully in v. 16, *Let the word of Christ dwell in you richly in all wisdom.* The parallel passage in Eph. 5:18 puts it another way, *Be filled with the Spirit*. God will never force you to be filled. You must choose it and ask Him to fill you, believing He has done it the very moment you ask. Are you appropriating His power over sin? If the very basic matters of putting off and putting on are not the normal experience of your life, then how can you expect to have His power for greater aspects of Christian life and growth, such as power for ministry and power over the devil?

Power for Ministry

Not surprisingly, the Holy Spirit who indwells us is the divine means by which we obtain power for ministry.

> And he said unto them, Which of you shall have a friend, and shall go unto him at midnight, and say unto him, Friend, lend me three loaves; For a friend of mine in his journey is come to me, and I have nothing to set before him? And he from within shall answer and say, Trouble me not: the door is now shut, and my children are with me in bed; I cannot rise and give thee. I say unto you, Though he will not rise and give him, because he is his friend, yet because of his importunity he will rise and give him as many as he needeth. Luke 11:5-8

When considering this parable, it is important to understand a Middle Eastern custom that was not only prominent during the time of Jesus but also continues to this day in that region of the world. When guests are being entertained in a Middle Eastern home, the cultural expectation is that the host will provide an abundance of food, drink, lodging and even conversation.

In this parable a guest shows up at midnight — of all times! Nevertheless, cultural considerations obligate the host to provide for his guest's needs. In this parable, the host is unprepared and so goes to his friend, perhaps a neighbor, at that late hour to borrow some bread. The neighbor's first response is, "Go away! It's late and we're all in bed." However, because of the host's importunity, or continued asking, the neighbor gets out of bed and loans his friend as much bread as he needs to feed the unexpected guest. In the end, the needs are met, albeit reluctantly. The spiritual application is clear, because Jesus states it plainly in the following verses:

And I say unto you, Ask, and it shall be given you; seek, and ye shall find; knock, and it shall be opened unto you. For every one that asketh receiveth; and he that seeketh findeth; and to him that knocketh it shall be opened. If a son shall ask bread of any of you that is a father, will he give him a stone? or if he ask a fish, will he for a fish give him a serpent? Or if he shall ask an egg, will he offer him a scorpion? If ye then, being evil, know how to give good gifts unto your children: how much more shall your heavenly Father give the Holy Spirit to them that ask him? Luke 11:9-13

Having now seen the parable and its spiritual application, we can make three observations.

Observation #1: The purpose for asking is because a friend has a need and we are destitute of ourselves to meet the need. Whether saved or lost, people need bread for their hungry souls. Jesus is the Bread of Life. Those who eat of His bread never hunger. We have no bread of ourselves to offer to others, so we must go to the Lord, asking Him to provide the Bread of Life that is needed. Yes, we have the Word of God and that is a critical component in ministry. But we also need His power for ministering to others. We need our Lord to breathe life on His Word as we are sharing it so the listener's ears and eyes will be opened to truth.

In the passage, the bread is not merely a reference to the Word, for when we ask our heavenly Father for "bread" for ministry, He doesn't give the Word, per se. He gives the Holy Spirit, according to v. 13. Thus, our need is for the Holy Spirit to breathe life upon our ministry to others, whether preaching to an audience or teaching in a classroom or speaking one-to-one, such as in witnessing and discipleship. When we ask, He always answers by providing the enabling power of the Holy Spirit.

Dare we try to minister without Him? Many do, which means their ministry is of the flesh — perhaps with enticing words of man's wisdom — but, consequently, lacking in power and effectiveness. Ministry in the flesh is ineffective and can even be counterproductive. Oh, how we must recognize our inadequacy to meet the needs of ourselves! The apostle Paul said, *Not that we are sufficient of ourselves to think any thing as of ourselves; but our sufficiency is of God;* 2 Cor. 3:5.

Some may argue that since all Christians have the Holy Spirit living within, there is no need to ask for Him. That leads to a second observation:

Observation #2: The request is for Holy Spirit empowering, not for the Person of the Spirit. In the Greek, the definite article is absent before the words *Holy Spirit* in the original language. When that is the case in Greek, then the reference is to the *essence* or *operation* or *nature* of the person or thing rather than its identity. In other words, Luke here, using very precise language, is not referring to the *Person* of the Holy Spirit but rather to His *ministry* of helping and empowering. That brings great meaning to this promise for disciples of all ages

Observation #3. The answer is always granted to those who ask in faith. God promises in v. 13, *How much more shall your heavenly Father give the Holy Spirit to them that ask Him?* What Jesus is promising is that whenever we ask God for Holy Spirit empowering, our heavenly Father will give it. This means that empowering is not automatic, though it is always available, through the Spirit who lives within us. God wants us to demonstrate our humble dependence on Him by asking for power rather than assuming we have it. Perhaps if we did not have to ask, we would tend to grow self-sufficient, thinking power is inherently at our disposal.

What are we to do with promises? We are to claim them, believe them. If we truly believe this promise, then the moment we ask, we should consider it done. Take it by faith, for God — who has promised — cannot lie. He must fulfill His word. He will give power for ministry when we ask in faith. How, then, does the idea of importunity factor into this parable?

Importunity, as presented in the parable, may give the impression of an arm-twisting, pestering mentality that won't stop until it gets what it wants. Is this what Jesus was teaching — a "squeaky-wheel-gets-the-grease" philosophy of prayer? God forbid! Where's the faith in that? That kind of praying suggests the more one pesters God, the more likely he is to get an answer. That may be the case in the *parable* — beating on the neighbor's door at midnight — but not in the *application*: asking God for Holy Spirit power and boldness for ministry.

In other words, Jesus presents a stark contrast between *man's* response to asking and *His* response to asking. Notice four points of difference.

Contrast between Man's Response and God's Response

First, the neighbor in the parable is asleep and must be awakened, whereas God never slumbers or sleeps. He is always alert to our requests. He never rebukes us for asking, nor does He refuse to answer. He is always ready and willing.

Second, the parable poses a friend-neighbor (peer) relationship, whereas with God we have a Father-child (family) relationship (the point of v. 13). If a neighbor will reluctantly loan his friend some bread after much arm-twisting, and if a sinful, earthly father will eventually fulfill the persistent requests of his children, *how much more* will God freely give His own children Holy Spirit empowering when they ask for it in faith?

Third, in the parable the expectation is that the bread is a loan from the neighbor; it will need to be repaid. However, with God, His bestowal of the Holy Spirit's enabling power is graciously given, granted out of His gracious heart.

Fourth, the neighbor in the parable has made his friend no promises to loan bread when needed, but God has promised to empower us with His Spirit whenever we ask.

The contrast is vivid between man and God. Man must often be pestered before reluctantly meeting needs, but not God. Indeed, it would be rank unbelief for us to pester God for His power when He has already promised it. To be sure, there is a continued asking implied in vs. 9 and 10. The Greek verbs *ask*, *seek*, and *knock* are in the present tense, which means continued action (*keep* asking, *keep* seeking, *keep* knocking). But this is not importunate arm-twisting or vain repetition. To continue asking, seeking and knocking is simply coming to God every time we need His power for ministry. We don't ask once and expect to have His power for the rest of our lives. Nor do we ask repeatedly to obtain His power for the immediate situation at hand.

Will God Always Answer?

Incidentally, is it possible to ask for God's power and not get it? Absolutely, there are at least four conditions that could result in God not answering your request for His power:

First, if you have sin in your life. In that case, you are not a candidate for receiving the Spirit's power. Instead, you need to learn to walk in the Spirit and not fulfill the lusts of the flesh.

Second, if you fail to see your own insufficiency. The host in the parable has the attitude, *I have nothing* (v. 6), and thus he receives bread, but a self-sufficient attitude will result in forfeiture of God's power. God resists the proud but gives grace to the humble (James 4:6).

Third, if you selfishly want power merely for the sake of power, to be recognized as some kind of super saint, not for the purpose of ministering to others. In the parable, the host needs bread to feed a friend, not for himself.

Fourth, if you fail to depend upon God's promise in faith, your prayer will not be answered, for the implication of v. 13 is one who asks in faith.

Virtually every time I am about to preach or minister to others in some way, I pray quietly in this fashion. "Lord, I need your bread for hungry people now. Please empower me with your Spirit, as you have promised. I take you at your Word." I don't pray numerous times, just once. Then I go forward with complete confidence, knowing He has answered. Tomorrow, I will pray the same, when needed, and again the next day and the next, and so on. When I ask on His terms, He always demonstrates power through my life, and I know it's not of me. Praise the Lord for His promise of empowering!

In the Christian life, we find another type of power that needs to be appropriated by children of God, and it touches on the weighty matter of spiritual warfare.

Power over the Enemy

Believers are admonished to *seek those things which are above, where Christ sitteth on the right hand of God*, Col. 3:1. The image of Christ sitting at the right hand of God conveys a place of magnificent power and authority. We are to seek power from the throne of the universe. Our Lord intends for us to appropriate *His* power, *His* authority, over the enemy. We see this truth emphasized once again in the epistle to the Ephesians.

> 19 That ye may know ... what is the exceeding greatness of his power to us-ward who believe, according to the working of his mighty power,
> 20 which he wrought in Christ, when he raised him from the dead, and set him at his own right hand in the heavenly places,
> 21 far above all principality, and power, and might, and dominion, and every name that is named, not only in this world, but also in that which is to come:
> 22 And hath put all things under his feet, and gave him to be the head over all things to the church. Eph. 1:19-22

In the Greek text behind v. 19, we find not merely one, but four words that express God's mighty power on behalf of the saints: *power* (*dunamis*), *working* (*energeia*), *mighty* (*ischus*), *power* (*kratos*). Furthermore, the words are accentuated by two adjectives, *exceeding greatness*. Considering the definitions of all words involved, the sentence could read as follows. God wants us to know what is the surpassing magnitude of His miracle-working power, the energizing, effectual, life-giving, forcefulness of His might.

What tremendous power we have at our disposal in the heavenlies! It is the power that raised Christ from the dead. It is the very power that comes from the throne room of God, where Christ is seated at the Father's right hand, the place of all authority. In fact, it is described in v. 21 as being *far above* all principality, power, might and dominion. In other words, His power is *far above* any other power imaginable, including the powers of man and Satan and the angelic realm, both now and in the future. God put all other powers under the feet of Christ, symbolizing their submission to His authority. The good news gets even more exciting.

> But God, who is rich in mercy, for his great love wherewith he loved us, even when we were dead in sins, hath quickened us together with Christ, (by grace ye are saved;) and hath raised us

up together, and made us sit together in heavenly places in Christ
Jesus. Eph. 2:4-6

At the point of initial salvation, you were seated with
Christ in the heavenlies, at the right hand of the Father. As we
have already seen, there is power at His throne, and all other
powers are under His feet. By way of your position in Christ,
you possess His delegated authority over the enemy. It is not
that all powers are under *your* feet, but they are under *His* feet,
and you are *in Him*. What that means is you have power over
the enemy through Christ. There is no power on Heaven or
Earth that can defeat you, when you recognize and claim your
position of authority in Him. Needless to say, no one should
ever become arrogant about this exalted position, because the
power belongs to God, not to man.

So few appropriate the throne-seat power of Christ, and
they are missing out on God's eternal purpose for their lives.

The Fellowship of the Mystery

I was made a minister ... that I should preach among the Gentiles
the unsearchable riches of Christ; and to make all men see what is
the fellowship of the mystery, which from the beginning of the
world hath been hid in God, who created all things by Jesus
Christ: to the intent that now unto the principalities and powers in
heavenly places might be known by the church the manifold
wisdom of God, according to the eternal purpose which he
purposed in Christ Jesus our Lord. Eph. 3:7-11

Now unto him that is able to do exceeding abundantly above all
that we ask or think, according to the power that worketh in us,
unto him be glory in the church by Christ Jesus throughout all
ages, world without end. Amen. Eph. 3:20-21

One key aspect of Paul's God-given ministry was to declare the *fellowship of the mystery*. A mystery, in the Bible sense,
is something hidden but now revealed. In Eph. 3 we learn that
God, in His multi-faceted wisdom, initiated a mystery in
eternity past and kept it concealed until it could be declared to
the church and then broadcast by the church to principalities
and powers in heavenly places — that is, the spirit world.

I have come to the conclusion that the *mystery* is not
merely the church — Jew and Gentile one in Christ —

although that is certainly part of the mystery. The mystery is much deeper than that. From the above passage in Ephesians, we find the mystery dates back, at least in our chronological way of thinking, before the beginning of the world. In advance of the Grand Plan (as we noted in Chapter 1) — God's creation of the world, despite knowing man would fall — He resolved in His eternal purpose not only to send His only begotten Son to redeem fallen mankind and defeat the devil, but also to be glorified by reclaiming fallen creation and ruling together with His faithful firstborn sons in His kingdom. As we have already stated earlier in this book, Christ is ultimately glorified, not merely by going to the cross and rising again from the grave, and then being exalted at the right hand of the Father, as glorious as those truths are. Christ is glorified by bringing many sons unto glory who will be His co-regents. Indeed, God continued with the Grand Plan, even though He knew the devastating short-term result, so that ultimately Christ would be glorified as the ruler over all things. From our perspective, that is yet future.

In light of this truth, Paul's ministry emphasis was helping all men to see what is the *fellowship* of the mystery, the critical importance of believers entering into partnership or participation with that mystery, now revealed. That should also be our ministry emphasis. Unfortunately, it seems that very few believers and local church ministries are focused on the coming kingdom of Christ, and making necessary preparations in their lives for qualifying to rule with Him. They assume that by possessing the gift of eternal life, they are already qualified to reign with Him by default. That is incorrect, as explained earlier, and it is a tragedy, for those who believe in that manner have not entered into the fellowship of the mystery. They have failed to understand the means by which Christ is ultimately glorified.

The quintessential mystery is not just leading people to a saving knowledge of Jesus to become part of His church, which is the dominant focus of many ministries. It is progressing in sanctification, going all the way with Christ in discipleship, becoming an overcomer who will be rewarded at the Judgment Seat. To emphasize once again, the fellowship of the mystery is not merely "getting people saved" so they can go to Heaven when they die. That is the starting point, to be sure, but it is stopping short of the goal. Jesus loves saving lost people from eternal condemnation. But that is not what glorifies Him in the most ultimate sense. Christ is ultimately glorified when faithful saints enter into the fellowship of the mystery — by cooperating and partnering with Jesus in their sufferings *now*, so they can be His co-heirs *then*. It is the duty of the church to make this manifold wisdom of God known, not only to the peoples of the world, but to the realm of the angels, particularly Satan's realm. The church needs to broadcast not merely the gospel of salvation from eternal condemnation, but also the gospel of Satan's demise and overthrow by King Jesus and his co-regents. After all, that is God's eternal purpose.

Eye Hath Not Seen Nor Ear Heard

> 6 Howbeit we speak wisdom among them that are perfect: yet not the wisdom of this world, nor of the princes of this world, that come to nought:
> 7 But we speak the wisdom of God in a mystery, even the hidden wisdom, which God ordained before the world unto our glory:
> 8 Which none of the princes of this world knew: for had they known it, they would not have crucified the Lord of glory.
> 9 But as it is written, Eye hath not seen, nor ear heard, neither have entered into the heart of man, the things which God hath prepared for them that love him. 1 Cor. 2:6-9

Paul had a deeper message for mature saints, for he said, *we speak wisdom among them that are perfect* (i.e., mature in the Lord). He describes this wisdom as a *mystery ... which God ordained before the world unto our glory*. This is the fellowship of the mystery that Paul mentions in Eph. 3 and, once again, it involves saints partnering with Christ through endurance in suffering, with the goal of being glorified in the future.

Now take special note as to what Paul says about the princes of this world. Had they known this hidden wisdom, this mystery, they would not have crucified Christ. I believe that the *princes of this world* in v. 8 would be a reference to Satan and his realm. Think of it! Had Satan known God had ordained before the world hidden wisdom — the fellowship of the mystery — unto our *glory* (i.e., faithful saints ruling with Jesus), then he would never have pushed for the crucifixion of the Lord of glory. For little did Satan realize at the time that the crucifixion, followed by the resurrection, was the watershed moment in history that makes possible, not only the redemption of mankind, but the glories of Jesus co-reigning with His faithful bride in the New Jerusalem. Furthermore, Satan now realizes — though he did not at Calvary — that all creation is moving toward the grand purpose of God, and that is the deposing of Satan and his rule over this world system in this age, to be replaced by human rulers, those who are the sons being led unto glory.

Thus, Paul could quote the prophet Isaiah in saying, *Eye hath not seen, nor ear heard, neither have entered into the heart of man, the things which God hath prepared for them that love him.* Notice, God has prepared these marvelous things of glory for those who love Him. These things of glory are not being prepared for all saints, but only for those who love Him; perhaps it could be said, for those who fellowship in His mystery, those who fellowship in His sufferings.

Of Which Salvation the Prophets Inquired

> 3 Blessed be the God and Father of our Lord Jesus Christ, which according to his abundant mercy hath begotten us again unto a lively hope by the resurrection of Jesus Christ from the dead,
> 4 To an inheritance incorruptible, and undefiled, and that fadeth not away, reserved in heaven for you,
> 5 Who are kept by the power of God through faith unto salvation ready to be revealed in the last time.
> 6 Wherein ye greatly rejoice, though now for a season, if need be, ye are in heaviness through manifold temptations:
> 7 That the trial of your faith, being much more precious than of gold that perisheth, though it be tried with fire, might be found unto praise and honour and glory at the appearing of Jesus Christ:
> 8 Whom having not seen, ye love; in whom, though now ye see him not, yet believing, ye rejoice with joy unspeakable and full of glory:
> 9 Receiving the end of your faith, even the salvation of your souls.
> 10 Of which salvation the prophets have enquired and searched diligently, who prophesied of the grace that should come unto you:
> 11 Searching what, or what manner of time the Spirit of Christ which was in them did signify, when it testified beforehand the sufferings of Christ, and the glory that should follow.

12 Unto whom it was revealed, that not unto themselves, but unto us they did minister the things, which are now reported unto you by them that have preached the gospel unto you with the Holy Ghost sent down from heaven; which things the angels desire to look into. 1 Pet. 1:3-12

According to this text, we have been saved for a purpose — and what is the purpose? That we might obtain *an inheritance incorruptible, undefiled and that fadeth not away, reserved in heaven*, v. 4. But that is not the inheritance of all saints. All saints possess the gift of eternal life, but not all saints possess an eternal reward. As v. 5 indicates, the inheritance (reward) reserved in Heaven is only for those saints who are kept (preserved) by the power of God through faith unto (future) salvation. Peter is not speaking of past salvation of one's spirit from eternal condemnation. He is speaking of future salvation of one's soul, which is the matter of reward at the Judgment Seat. Here's how you obtain that kind of inheritance: by responding rightly to your trials as Christ did to His, so that you *might be found unto praise and honor and glory* at His appearing (v. 7). Again, that is not the future for all saints, only a faithful subset. If you are faithful, as v. 9 says, you will receive the *end* of your faith, even the salvation of your soul (reward) at the Judgment Seat.

This soul-salvation, v. 10, is what the prophets did not fully understand, perhaps only getting a mere glimpse of the concept, for it was a mystery. In v. 11 we are told they searched the matter of Christ's sufferings and *the glory that should follow*. The matter of Christ's sufferings is prophesied to some extent in the Old Testament (e.g., Isa. 53; Ps. 22). But the matter of *the glory that should follow* — glory for Jesus as well as glory for those who suffer with Him — was not revealed very much, except for some hints here and there, until New Testament times.

The Curious Angels

Interestingly, the end of v. 12 says the angels desire to look into these things. What *things*? Perhaps you have heard it said that the angels are curious about the gospel, because they can't be saved. That could be, but I can't imagine that is what

Peter is saying here, because the context is referring to future soul-salvation not past spirit-salvation. I believe the reason the angels — particularly Satan's spirit realm — are so curious is because they realize they will one day be deposed and replaced by qualified, glorified men who will rule in their stead. They desire to look into this matter because it affects their future. Undoubtedly, the holy angels are desirous to see sons led unto glory, and to that end, they are ministering on behalf of those who will become inheritors of soul-salvation (see Heb. 1:14). The devil and his evil angels, on the other hand, want to derail sons from being led unto glory, and so Satan walks about as a roaring lion *seeking whom he may devour*, 1 Pet. 5:8. That understanding helps to explain Satan's agenda in the present age.

Dear child of God, if you want to inherit the glory that comes from soul-salvation, then you must obey Peter's admonition.

> Wherefore gird up the loins of your mind, be sober, and hope to the end for the grace that is to be brought unto you at the revelation of Jesus Christ; as obedient children, not fashioning yourselves according to the former lusts in your ignorance: but as he which hath called you is holy, so be ye holy in all manner of conversation; because it is written, Be ye holy; for I am holy. 1 Pet. 1:13-16

On that glorious note, let us return to Eph. 1 and close the chapter by discussing how we appropriate our throne-seat authority.

Appropriating Throne Seat Authority

You are seated with Christ in the heavenlies. You have at your disposal His delegated authority over the Satanic realm. To the extent that you appropriate Christ's power for victory over the enemy *now*, you will be qualified and prepared to rule over angels *then*. How, then, do we appropriate His power over the enemy?

> That ye may know ... what is the exceeding greatness of his power to us-ward who believe, according to the working of his mighty power. Eph. 1:18-19

The exceeding greatness of His power is only appropriated by those *who believe*. It is not referring to *all* saints (whom we sometimes refer to as *believers*). It is referring to *believing* saints, those saints who are depending on the Master to give them power for defeating the enemy. Yet so few believe, so few appropriate the power. I believe that could be one of the key reasons Christ has not yet returned — because He has not led enough sons unto glory. Of course, it is not because He is unable; it is because His children are unwilling. He will not force it upon anyone; the power is for those who believe, for those who depend on Him to do it.

John MacMillan, who wrote an outstanding book called, *The Authority of the Believer*, (p. 21-22) said:

> Why, then, is there not more manifest progress? Because a head is wholly dependent upon its body for the carrying out of its plan. All the members of its body must be subservient, that through their coordinated ministry may be accomplished what is purposed. The Lord Jesus, "Head over all things to the Church, which is His body" (Ephesians 1:22-23), is hindered in His mighty plans and working, because His Body has failed to appreciate the deep meaning of His exaltation and to respond to the gracious impulses which He is constantly sending for its quickening. [23]

My heart breaks to hear that, but it is true. Oh for men and women who will submit to the Head and depend on Him for the power to defeat the enemy both temporally and eternally! Oh for saints of God who will learn to resist the devil! Are you magnifying Christ by appropriating His power over sin, power for ministry, and power over the enemy?

---

[23] John A. MacMillan, *The Authority of the Believer* (Camp Hill, PA: Wingspread Publishers/Zur Ltd., 2007), 21-22.

Chapter 8

Exhibiting Eternal Glory

The lighthouse at Alexandria was one of the seven won-
ders of the ancient world. Constructed in the third century BC,
historians now believe it could have towered up to four hundred fifty feet in height.[24] Located on the Mediterranean port
city of Alexandria, it provided an important warning for
mariners approaching the coast. The light was reflected out to
sea by use of a mirror, guiding ships safely into harbor.
Modern lighthouses still use reflectors for broadcasting light,
as well as refracting lenses that magnify.[25] The intense beacon
light emitted from the tower is powerful and attention getting.

Christians are to be lighthouses too, reflecting and
refracting the glory of Jesus in our sin-cursed world, so that
others can see His brightness in our lives as He is magnified.
Jesus admonished, *Let your light so shine before men, that they
may see your good works, and glorify your Father which is in
heaven*, Matt. 5:16. Think of it, we are to be beacons of light,
radiating with the glow of the Savior and thereby exhibiting
eternal glory!

**Christ is magnified when you reflect His glory by your
life and thereby become transformed into His image in ever-
increasing measures of glory.**

1 If ye then be risen with Christ, seek those things which are above, where Christ sitteth on the right hand of God.
2 Set your affection on things above, not on things on the earth.
3 For ye are dead, and your life is hid with Christ in God.
4 When Christ, who is our life, shall appear, then shall ye also appear with him in glory. Col. 3:1-4

What does it mean to *appear* with Christ in glory? And what is *glory*? The purpose of this chapter is to answer these important questions, but the answer may not be what you are expecting.

Unconditional and Conditional

In the passage above we find both an unconditional statement and a conditional statement. The unconditional is not seen as clearly in English as it is in Greek. For instance, notice v. 1 starts out with the word *if*, which may prompt the reader to think it is a conditional statement — *If you do this; then God will do that*. But that is not the idea in the original language. The first word *if* could be translated *since*. Paul is writing to an audience of saints who already died with Christ and rose with Him at the point of initial salvation. Thus, v. 1 could legitimately read, *Since you are risen with Christ*, and v. 3 could read, *For you died*. All believers died with Christ when saved and rose with Him too. That is the provision for living victoriously, a doctrinal truth mapped out in detail in Rom. 6-8. Your death and resurrection with Christ are unconditional.

Next comes the conditional part, and it's clearly conditional, for it's given in the form of a command, and not all Christians obey this command. The condition is *if* you will seek those things which are above, *if* you will set your affection on things above, not on earthly things — in other words, *if* you have an eternal worldview — *then* when Christ, your life, appears, you will also appear with Him in glory. The glorious benefit of v. 4 is conditioned on your obedience to the command in vs. 1-2. If you choose not to seek things above and if you choose not to set your affection on things above rather than on earthly things, then you will not appear with Him in glory. Putting it another way, if you want to appear with Him in glory, then you need to do what is commanded in vs. 1-2.

What is glory?

There is a tendency in the minds of some Christians to see the word *glory* and subconsciously insert the word *Heaven*, at least in this passage. In other words, they tend to think v. 4 is an unconditional statement suggesting that when Christ returns, we will go to be with Him in glory, in *Heaven*. However, while Heaven is glorious, to be sure, the word *glory* here does not refer to Heaven.

Glory Defined

> Whether therefore ye eat, or drink, or whatsoever ye do, do all to the glory of God. 1 Cor. 10:31

The word *glory* is used as a noun in the above verse, and in a noun sense glory is a good opinion concerning someone, resulting in praise and honor. In a verb sense, 1 Cor. 6:20 admonishes that because the Holy Spirit lives within, you are to *glorify God in your body, and in your spirit, which are God's* — that is, bring Him praise and honor by the way you live your life. If you do, then He will glorify you. However, Jesus will not bestow His glory on those saints who choose to live ingloriously.

Conditions for Being Glorified

In several places in the Scriptures we find Christ glorifies those saints who meet His conditions.

> And if children, then heirs; heirs of God, and joint-heirs with Christ; if so be that we suffer with him, that we may be also glorified together. Rom. 8:17

The condition for being glorified is suffering with Him; that is, responding rightly amidst our sufferings, a topic we explored extensively in a previous chapter.

> For whom he did foreknow, he also did predestinate to be conformed to the image of his Son, that he might be the firstborn among many brethren. Moreover whom he did predestinate, them he also called: and whom he called, them he also justified: and whom he justified, them he also glorified. Rom. 8:29-30

The condition for being glorified is becoming conformed to the image of His Son. According to Col. 3:4, quoted earlier, the condition for being glorified is seeking those things that are above and setting your affection on them. Only those saints who meet the conditions will be glorified with Him.

Glory Can Be Seen

Glory is manifested visibly in the form of brightness. It is shining, a glow of sorts. After Moses completed the building of the tabernacle in Exod. 40, the glory of the Lord filled the place, and Moses could not enter because of it. The Shekinah glory emanated from the ark of the covenant in the holy of holies, for God dwelt there. In 2 Chron. 6, when Solomon dedicated the temple to the Lord, the children of Israel saw the glory of the Lord fill the place. In Luke 2, when the angel of the Lord appeared to the shepherds out in the fields, *The glory of the Lord shone round about them*, Luke 2:9. In Acts 7, when Stephen was being stoned to death, he looked up into Heaven and saw the glory of God. In Rev. 18:1, an angel will descend from Heaven during the tribulation, and the whole earth will become lightened by his glory.

This implies that God does not keep glory to Himself. He shares it with His created beings, including holy angels. From passages shared earlier in the chapter, we know He also shares His glory with those of His brethren who are living in holiness. We have no glory of our own, but Christ is delighted to share His glory with us. But He only shares His glory with those who are living gloriously. In the Col. 3 text, the conditions are laid out in vs. 1-2, and in vs. 5-25. The entire passage cannot be quoted here, but I would recommend you read it in your Bible and notice especially vs. 23-25:

> 23 And whatsoever ye do, do it heartily, as to the Lord, and not unto men;

24 Knowing that of the Lord ye shall receive the reward of the inheritance: for ye serve the Lord Christ.
25 But he that doeth wrong shall receive for the wrong which he hath done: and there is no respect of persons. Col. 3:23-25

The reward of the inheritance is appearing with Christ in glory (v. 4), which God will bestow only upon faithful saints. According to v. 25, unfaithful saints will get something too. It is not that they will be unrewarded; the verse specifically says they will receive for their wrongdoing. What will they receive? To answer that question, we must go on a quest.

Glorified Bodies ... or Not

35 But some man will say, How are the dead raised up? and with what body do they come?
36 Thou fool, that which thou sowest is not quickened, except it die:
37 And that which thou sowest, thou sowest not that body that shall be, but bare grain, it may chance of wheat, or of some other grain:
38 But God giveth it a body as it hath pleased him, and to every seed his own body.
39 All flesh is not the same flesh: but there is one kind of flesh of men, another flesh of beasts, another of fishes, and another of birds.
40 There are also celestial bodies, and bodies terrestrial: but the glory of the celestial is one, and the glory of the terrestrial is another.
41 There is one glory of the sun, and another glory of the moon, and another glory of the stars: for one star differeth from another star in glory.
42 So also is the resurrection of the dead. 1 Cor. 15:35-42

The tendency by many is to assume from Paul's discourse on bodily resurrection that all saints will receive a glorified body when they meet Christ. But is that what this passage is teaching? It seems he is anticipating rhetorical questions from his intended audience: *How are the dead raised up? With what body do they come? v. 35.*

The answer first comes by way of illustration in vs. 36-37. The bodies of saints are likened to bare grain or seed. The Greek word translated *bare* is typically translated *naked* in the New Testament. In fact, out of the fifteen times the Greek word is used in the New Testament, this is the only time it is translated *bare*. Paul is trying to drive home a point. Your body, though you can fix it up with fancy clothing and make-up and jewelry and hairstyles, etc., is merely like a naked seed in God's eyes. He knows the real *you*. *All things are naked and opened unto the eyes of him with whom we have to do*, Heb. 4:13.

At the resurrection God will retool the bodies of saints to function in the ethereal, eternal realm, which I believe is a world of higher dimensions. At that time, He will determine what kind of body each person receives, *as it hath pleased Him*, v. 38. From the start we get the idea that not all bodies will be alike in essence, and vs. 39-42 seem to corroborate that notion. What determines the kind of body God will bestow upon each saint? Jesus apparently answered that question.

> 23 Jesus answered them, saying, The hour is come, that the Son of man should be glorified.
> 24 Verily, verily, I say unto you, Except a corn of wheat fall into the ground and die, it abideth alone: but if it die, it bringeth forth much fruit.
> 25 He that loveth his life shall lose it; and he that hateth his life in this world shall keep it unto life eternal. John 12:23-25

Paul's analogy of a body as a bare seed is not original. Jesus first employed that imagery in the Gospels. In the most immediate sense, the seed is referring to the body of Christ being crucified and buried, going into the ground and dying. The Father resurrected His Son, initially giving Him a resurrected body that can function in the eternal realm — as seen when Jesus instantaneously appeared and disappeared to His disciples and to those on the road to Emmaus. But because of His obedience to the will of the Father and Christ's endurance in suffering, He also has been exalted and will one day receive a glorified body — to be distinguished from His mere resurrected body — as glimpsed on the Mt. of Transfiguration. It is a body of intense brightness and beauty.

How does this apply to us? *Christ the firstfruits; afterward they that are Christ's at his coming*, 1 Cor. 15:23. All saints will apparently receive a resurrected body, presumably at the rapture. The assumption by many, however, is that all saints will also receive a glorified body. But according to the illustration used by Jesus in John 12 — and reiterated by Paul in 1 Cor. 15

— it seems that saints will only be glorified if they go into the ground and die, metaphorically speaking. Of course, all saints have died with Christ in a *positional* sense, as described in Chapter 2, but the qualification described by Jesus is death to self in a *practical, experiential* sense. It is the idea of hating your life (soul) in this world so that you keep it (i.e., find that you are rewarded at the Judgment Seat) unto life eternal (v. 24). *Life eternal* in this verse is not referring to the *gift* of eternal life, possessed by all, but rather to the *reward* of eternal life, a quality of life in the age to come that is only granted to those who choose to die to self in this life. Incidentally, we know Jesus was not speaking about the matter of salvation from eternal condemnation in John 12. Salvation is not obtained by hating our life — that is, by *doing* something — which is a matter of sanctification. Rather, we are saved by faith alone, believing on the Lord Jesus Christ, not by works.

What, then, is the pathway to glorification? It is choosing to die to self, hating your life in this world, so that in a spiritual sense you go into the ground like a naked seed and die. If you do, then in the resurrection, God will give you a measure of glory, as it pleases Him. It is as if Paul is saying, "Don't you remember what Jesus said?" The implication of this text is that the nature of your resurrection body will be determined according to whether you die spiritually in this life or not.

Continuing into vs. 39-41, Paul uses an illustration from nature to discuss the prospect of various kinds of bodies in the resurrection. Just as men have one kind of flesh, mammals another, fish another, and birds yet another — and just as the celestial bodies (sun, moon, stars) differ greatly in their intensity — so also is the resurrection of the dead (v. 42). In other words, resurrected bodies will vary greatly. In fact, just as celestial bodies are greater in glory than terrestrial bodies (v. 40), so our resurrected body will be greater in glory than our present physical body. Furthermore, just as there are different types of celestial bodies, having different intensities (v. 41), so in the resurrection there will be differing types of glorified bodies, varying in intensity of glory. The logical conclusion is that some resurrected saints will glow more brightly than others, for glory has to do with brightness, as we noted earlier. Is that not evident from Christ's transfiguration?

Returning to Col. 3:24, we can now answer the question, what is the reward of the inheritance? At least in part, it is a degree of glory that is bestowed upon a faithful saint. What, then, does it mean in v. 25 that some saints will receive according to their wrongdoing? Does it simply mean they will not be rewarded? No, it seems in the context of Col. 3:4 that they will not be glorified. They will receive only a resurrected body, not a glorified one. Like the bare seed, they will be naked — not clothed with glory — and that will bring shame.

Clothed in His Brightness or Naked and Ashamed?

Here's a marvelous thought. Adam and Eve were clothed with glory (brightness) before the fall. That was their clothing. But when they sinned, they lost the clothing of brightness, their glory. That is how they became naked and ashamed, necessitating that God kill animals in order to clothe Adam with the skins. The blood of the animals was a type of the blood of the spotless Lamb of God that that would be shed for the sins of the whole world. When Jesus — the second Adam — won the victory over death and Satan at the cross and through His subsequent resurrection, He was glorified by the Father and highly exalted (cf. Phil. 2:9-11). In His coming kingdom He will be encased in brightness, and that is prefigured for us in the Transfiguration account (Matt. 17). Not only will Jesus be encased in brightness, so will the mature sons that He brings to *glory*. Thus, what happened to our primeval parents in the Garden — the loss of their glory as a covering — will be reversed at the Judgment Seat, when faithful saints will be clothed in brightness and given crowns (James 1:12), representing regality. The bare seed of those who go into the ground and die in this present world will be clothed with great glory in the next.

On the other hand, those who love their life now rather than hating it, will find at the Judgment Seat they will be ashamed. How will they be ashamed? They will not be given white robes of righteousness; they will not glow with bright-ness in any degree. They will possess only a resurrected body which, granted, is better than the present physical body, but they will remain, nonetheless, unclothed, naked and ashamed. Remember the parable Jesus shared about the man who showed up at the wedding feast without the proper garment (Matt. 22:12)? He could not join in the joys of the wedding feast because he was not properly clothed. The man was speechless. He could say nothing for himself; he was unclothed and ashamed. The king ordered the man to be removed to the darkness outside. (For a further discussion of outer darkness, see my book, *The End of the Pilgrimage.*).

Two Types of Saints

> 17 Brethren, be followers together of me, and mark them which walk so as ye have us for an ensample.
> 18 (For many walk, of whom I have told you often, and now tell you even weeping, that they are the enemies of the cross of Christ:
> 19 Whose end is destruction, whose God is their belly, and whose glory is in their shame, who mind earthly things.)
> 20 For our conversation is in heaven; from whence also we look for the Saviour, the Lord Jesus Christ:
> 21 Who shall change our vile body, that it may be fashioned like unto his glorious body, according to the working whereby he is able even to subdue all things unto himself. Phil. 3:17-21

We find in these verses two types of saints. Those who are living for self and earthly pleasures, destroying their lives, are seen in v. 18-19. They *mind earthly things.* What type of glory can they expect in the world to come? Their glory is *in their shame.* In other words, their resurrected body will be shameful, for they will not be endowed with the brightness of glory. Instead, they will be naked and ashamed. On the contrary, in v. 20-21 we find those whose citizenship is in Heaven, and by that I believe Paul (in this context) is referring to those who will be included in the heavenly New Jerusalem, reigning with Christ. What kind of glory can they expect in the world to come? Their *vile* body (i.e., body of low estate) will be conformed to Christ's body of glory. Another way of saying this is found in our opening text in Col. 3.

> When Christ, who is our life, shall appear, then shall ye also appear with him in glory. Col. 3:4

Appearing with Christ in Glory

The word *appear* is a verb. It means "to render apparent (literally or figuratively); to manifestly declare."[26] Thayer says *to appear* is "to make manifest or visible or known what has been hidden or unknown, to manifest, whether by words, or deeds, or in any other way."[27] Wuest points out that it is in the passive voice, which means the subject is not doing the action; the subject is being acted upon.[28] Thus, it could read, "When Christ is made to become manifest or visible."

Most commentators see the word *appear* in Col. 3:4 as eschatological, either referring to Christ's appearing at the rapture or the second coming. But must we arrive at that sole conclusion? Undoubtedly, it applies *ultimately* to the future and the prospect of the believer's reward at the Judgment Seat, but could it also be referring to a possibility in the Christian's life here and now? In the Greek, it is permissible. Let me explain.

We noted earlier in the chapter that v. 3 is an unconditional fact. When you were saved, you died with Christ, and your life was hidden with Christ in God. Secretly — in your innermost being, known only to you and to God — your life is now in Christ. The world can't see it, but you are saved. Your life is hidden with Christ in God. But when Christ, *your life* (v. 4), becomes manifest in your lifestyle — when what is hidden is made known — then you will also be made known with Him in glory. This could mean one of two things or, more likely, both. First, when Jesus who lives within you, is revealed in your life, here and now in this present world, then you will qualify to be glorified in the world to come. Second, it could also mean when Jesus who lives within you, is revealed in your life, here and now in this present world, He will glorify you even in this present age. This dual interpretation is entirely possible, as confirmed by another Scripture passage.

> But we all, with open face beholding as in a glass (reflecting as in a mirror) the glory of the Lord, are changed into the same image from glory to glory, even as by the Spirit of the Lord. 2 Cor. 3:18 (parenthesis added)

Whenever the veil is lifted from your hidden life with Christ, so that you magnify Him, reflecting His glory in this world, He transforms you into His image from glory to greater glory. It is like an upward spiral, picturing ever-increasing glory. That, I believe, is the secondary idea of Col. 3:4, and what a promise! My interpretation of the verse reads as follows:

> When our union with Christ — Christ our life, which is hidden — is rendered apparent, here and now, in the believer's life, through the believer's heavenly-minded manner of living (see vs. 1-2), then that believer will be rendered apparent together with Christ in glory.

If this interpretation is correct, then what is the qualification for being glorified? It is seeking those things that are above (v. 1) and setting your affection on things above (v. 2). Yet I would suggest that one of the tragedies of twenty-first century Christianity is that saints en masse are not even seeking Heaven, much less thinking Heaven. No doubt, there will be multitudes that will be ashamed when they stand before Jesus in judgment. They will go into the age to come in nakedness, with no glory, and they will be ashamed. May God deliver us from this awful condition and may we, by God's grace, exhibit eternal glory by reflecting the Savior.

---

[24] "Lighthouse of Alexandria," *Wikipedia: The Free Encyclopedia* (accessed Dec., 2015).

[25] "Fresnel Lens," *Wikipedia: The Free Encyclopedia* (accessed Dec., 2015).

[26] James Strong, *Strong's Exhaustive Greek Dictionary of the New Testament* (Nashville, TN: Crusade Bible Publ., no copyright), 75.

[27] Joseph H. Thayer, *Greek-English Lexicon of the New Testament*, online version, (accessed Dec. 2015), http://www.biblestudytools.com/lexicons/greek/phaneroo.

[28] Kenneth S. Wuest, *Wuest's Word Studies From the Greek New Testament* (Grand Rapids, MI: Wm. B. Eerdman's Publ. Co., 1953), vol. 1, "Ephesians and Colossians," 218.

Chapter 9

Grasping
Four-Dimensional Love

The Triplet of Faith, Hope and Love

Are faith, hope and love progressive realms of our Christian pilgrimage? It would seem so, according to the Scriptures. Certainly, we continue to experience growth in each of these areas throughout our Christian lives. However, there appears to be a progression in understanding from one realm to the next, starting with the most basic aspect of faith, then hope, and finally love. These three things are often mentioned in triplets in the Word of God. For instance, Paul reminisced about the work of faith and patience of hope and labor of love of the Thessalonian church (1 Thess. 1:3). In Rom. 5, a passage that describes the process of spiritual growth, we are admonished to access God's grace by *faith* and then to glory in tribulations, knowing that they work patience (endurance), which works experience (Christian character), which works *hope*. A believer full of hope is unashamed. The *love* of God is shed abroad, outpoured, in that heart by the Holy Spirit. At the end of the great love chapter, we read of faith and hope and love as the three things that abide or remain, the greatest of which is love (1 Cor. 13:13).

The faith-hope-love triplet is like the pair of trifocals I wear for optimal vision. The basic, corrective lens (the top level of the glasses) assists with my distance vision, primarily when driving. The bifocal (bottom level) helps me read clearly, and the trifocal (middle level) aids in arms-length computer work. All three levels of corrective vision are part of the same lens, but depending on which level I am peering through determines what is most in focus. So it is with the spiritual life. Faith, hope and love are all part of the same spiritual lenses, but each one focuses on a different aspect of the Christian life.

Faith is the most basic level, and that is why Peter admonishes, *Add to your faith*, 2 Pet. 1:5. It is learning to live in daily dependence on the Holy Spirit who lives within. When you consistently walk in the Spirit, you will be enabled to live according to the eternal realm, in obedience to the Lord. Progressing from faith to hope is like moving from regular glasses to bifocals. A whole new field of vision opens before your eyes and what was once blurry becomes clear. Hope doesn't replace faith; it is added to faith. Your spiritual vision can then accommodate both realms. Hope is joyful expectation, not only of Christ's return, but also of His reward, bringing consistent, spiritual optimism. Hope can visualize Christ's eternal kingdom and the faithful believer's regal participation in it. Incidentally, a believer who is not walking by faith will never have hope, but a believer who has hope also has faith.

Finally, maturing from hope to love is like advancing from bifocals to trifocals — adding a third level of vision and focus. Love is dependent on hope, and hope is dependent on faith. Where there is no faith or hope, there can be no real love. A spirit of Christlike love is sacrificial in giving, esteeming others better than self, and looking out for the well-being of others.

The Glorious Land of Love

Paul said love is the greatest, the ultimate, of the triplet. That being the case, we must assume faith and hope are lesser, not in importance, but lesser in maturity level. God's will is that His children progress from faith to hope to love. But one of the tragedies of Christianity is that such a small percentage of saints ever seem to understand and live in the very basic realm of faith — that is, depending on the Lord for victory — much less progress to the more mature levels of hope and love.

Perhaps you noticed that Chapters 1 through 4 in this book deal primarily with the matter of living by faith and Chapters 5 through 8 emphasize hope-living. The intent of Chapters 9 and 10 will be to view love out in the distance — like Moses standing on Mt. Nebo, viewing the Promised Land. I have stood on that spot in Jordan, and the view is breathtaking. In like manner, our brief tour of love will be truly remarkable to ponder. There we will see Jesus in all His glory. Dare any of us suggest we have arrived in that glorious land of love? Nay, but it's there for the possessing, and we must possess it! Let us move on, then, to the ultimate land of love.

> 14 For this cause I bow my knees unto the Father of our Lord Jesus Christ ...
> 16 that he would grant you, according to the riches of his glory, to be strengthened with might by his Spirit in the inner man;
> 17 that Christ may dwell in your hearts by faith; that ye, being rooted and grounded in love,
> 18 may be able to comprehend with all saints what is the breadth, and length, and depth, and height;
> 19 and to know the love of Christ, which passeth knowledge, that ye might be filled with all the fulness of God.
> 20 Now unto him that is able to do exceeding abundantly above all that we ask or think, according to the power that worketh in us,
> 21 unto him be glory in the church by Christ Jesus throughout all ages, world without end. Amen. Eph. 3:14, 16-21

Christ is magnified when you comprehend the breadth and length and depth and height of Christ's love, to the end that you are filled with all the fulness of God.

Paul prays what is, in my opinion, his most beautiful prayer in Eph. 3:14-21. In the prayer he requests something absolutely astounding, something that short-circuits our finite minds. I used to think Paul was praying for several different things here in this passage: to be strengthened with might; to have Christ dwell in the heart; to know the love of Christ; to be filled with all the fulness of God. But upon further investigation one finds in the Greek that each of these requests is preceded with *in order that*.[29] What that means is each one of these phrases is dependent on the previous one. Wiersbe says these four requests are like four parts to a telescope. "One request leads into the next one, and so on."[30]

Strengthened with Might

I now understand Paul was praying for one central thing, but it is such a complicated thing that it requires assistance to be able to grasp it in our lives. The *one thing* is the love of Christ, which seems to be the pinnacle of the prayer in v. 19. The apostle wants us to be overwhelmed with the love of Jesus, much like Moses seeing breathtaking views on Nebo. But in order to grasp Christ's love, we must first scale the mountain of faith and hope so we can see the love.

It is impossible for any believer to ascend in faith or advance on to hope apart from Christ. Our Lord must enable us with strength *in the inner man* (v. 16) if there will be any success in climbing. The inner man is the *spirit* of man, where the Spirit of God resides, and is therefore, the source of your power. The spirit is the realm of your provision. Paul prays that we might be strengthened with *might* in that realm of our being. The word *might* is *dunamis* in the Greek. From it, we get our English word *dynamite*. *Dunamis* is abundant, miraculous power. It's not strength you possess of yourself. It is God's supernatural power that He gives to you by His Spirit in your spirit. Those believers who are appropriating this strength will be filled with the Spirit and enabled to ascend the mountain. Stepping out of the Spirit's filling by sinning halts progress until the sin is confessed.

Then Paul adds another significant requirement in v. 17a: *that Christ may dwell in your hearts by faith*. Only those saints who are regularly walking in the Spirit can experience Christ dwelling in their hearts by faith. For Christ to dwell, which means to abide or remain, He must be made Lord of one's life. In other words, the believer must, by faith, continually access the provision of the Holy Spirit in order to experience patterns of victory. When that happens, the Godhead abides with the believer in a personal, experiential sense.

If a man love me, he will keep my words: and my Father will love him, and we will come unto him, and make our abode with him. John 14:23

To the extent the believer keeps submitting, by faith, Christ will continue to dwell in that believer's soul. The idea of His dwelling, in this context, is that Christ will be *at home* in the believer's personality.[31] Of course, His Spirit indwells *every* believer, but Christ is not *at home* in the lives of all saints, for many live selfishly and disobediently. Why would He be at *home* in those lives? Christ is only *at home* in the heart of a believer who is obedient and holy, one who is being strengthened with might by the Holy Spirit in the innermost being. When that is the case, the believer is a candidate for what comes next, the focal point of Paul's prayer: *That ye, being rooted and grounded in love, may be able to comprehend with all saints what is the breadth, and length, and depth, and height; and to know the love of Christ, which passeth knowledge*, vs. 17-19.

Moving Beyond Roots and Foundation

God's desire is that we would be able to comprehend the vastness of Christ's love. To that end, the apostle uses two metaphors — rooted in love and grounded in love. *Rooted in love* is an agricultural illustration. All Christians have roots in Christ's love. We have experienced it in some degree in His saving us from eternal condemnation (see John 3:16; Rom. 5:8). Nevertheless, roots are only the beginning. God desires a plant of love to grow up and flourish from those roots.

Grounded in love is an architectural picture, drawing upon the image of a building's foundation. All Christians have a love foundation, because of Christ. But a foundation is not a building; it's only the base of a building. God wants a building of love to be erected in our lives upon the foundation of love.

Unfortunately, multitudes of Christians never grow beyond the rudimentary aspects of rooted and grounded in love. Because Christ does not dwell in their hearts by faith, they remain content with a shallow understanding of Christ's love. But God has so much more in store for His children, if we will submit to His conditions as outlined in vs. 16-17. He wants us to know His love in a deeper, fuller way. We could refer to this as a flourishing plant of love, not mere roots; a completed building of love, not mere foundation. The idea is a mature, thriving understanding of Christ's love for us that spills over into love for others.

Incomprehensible Love

This is where it gets really exciting. The pinnacle of Paul's prayer is found in v. 19. God wants saints to know the love of Christ that passes knowledge. How can you possibly know something that is beyond knowing? How can you comprehend the incomprehensible? The answer is in v. 16. It is only when you appropriate Holy Spirit *dunamis* — divine enablement in your inner man, so that Christ is at home in your heart by faith. When this is a reality in your life, then God will give you something very special.

> But as it is written, Eye hath not seen, nor ear heard, neither have entered into the heart of man, the things which God hath prepared for them that love him. 1 Cor. 2:9

Those who love God will be given a special reward, prepared by God. It is not for all saints, but only for those who love Him — and those who love Him are those who keep His commandments (John 14:15). The only possible way to keep His commandments is choosing, by faith, to depend upon the Holy Spirit to enable obedience (Eph. 3:16-17). When that condition is fulfilled in our lives, God will reveal to us something special that He has prepared — something our eyes have never seen and our ears have never heard; something we have never considered in our wildest imaginings. What is it?

Love in Four Dimensions

In part, it is experiencing Christ's love four-dimensionally. It is comprehending *the breadth, and length, and depth, and height* of Christ's love (Eph. 3:18). *Breadth* is width. Consider the breadth of Christ's love for mankind. It is wide enough to save any and all who come to Him, on His terms, for salvation. Jew or Gentile, bond or free, male or female; all become one in Christ because of His great love. Next is the *length* of Christ's love. He saves and loves throughout time, in every era of history, because His love is enduring. Then ponder the *height* of Christ's love. He loves us into the heavenly realm, which means we are also loved by the Father. We need to marvel and learn more about each of these aspects of Christ's love. The Holy Spirit of God will develop our understanding when we are, by faith, inviting Christ to be at home in the soul.

But what is the meaning of the *depth* of His love? The songwriter penned these words:

> Into the heart of Jesus
> Deeper and deeper I go,
> Seeking to know the reason
> Why He should love me so,
> Why He should stoop to lift me
> Up from the miry clay,
> Saving my soul, making me whole,
> Though I had wandered away.[32]

How can we go deeper and deeper in love? This is the fourth dimension of love. Let me try to illustrate. If we take only width or only length, then we have a line, which is one-dimensional. If we take width and length together, we have a two dimensional object, such as a square. If we add height to width and length, we now have a three-dimensional object, such as a cube. But what happens when we add a fourth dimension — *depth*? To keep with the analogy of a one-dimensional line; a two-dimensional square; and a three-dimensional cube; a four-dimensional object in this series would be a tesseract.

> In geometry, the tesseract is the four-dimensional analog of the cube; the tesseract is to the cube as the cube is to the square. Just as the surface of the cube consists of 6 square faces, the hypersurface of the tesseract consists of 8 cubical cells.[33]

If this seems over your head, it is intended to be, and here's why. We were created as three-dimensional beings, but the spirit realm resides in other dimensions. We cannot now see those dimensions, though I'm convinced that one day we will. In fact, though it is mathematically proven and can be imagined to a degree, we cannot even fully grasp the concept of a fourth dimension. Yet scientists, mathematicians, and philosophers tell us there may be as many as twelve dimensions! Incidentally, we cannot completely represent a four-dimensional tesseract by drawing it in our three-dimensional world, because not all of it can be seen at the same time. We can only see the portion that enters our three-dimensional world.

Are you still confused? Good! That is natural when discussing this subject because it is beyond us. Suffice to say, that a supernatural being in the fourth dimension can see through us and through other objects in our three-dimensional world. When I look at you, I can only see the front side of you, because I am limited. If I want to see the backside of you, I have to move around behind you. That is why we use mirrors — to help us see other sides of us that are beyond our view. Now imagine living in a world of mirrors, so to speak. Not an illusory world, but a real world, in which you can see all sides of everything at the same time. That is a four-dimensional world. Then imagine if you also had the ability to see through people into their inside as well as their outside at the same time. That is a four-dimensional world. To be sure, it is mind boggling, and I don't begin to understand it all, for it is incomprehensible. Nevertheless, the point is this. The Word of God tells us, very explicitly, that we can reach a point in our spiritual lives where we can comprehend the incomprehensible. We can actually comprehend the fourth dimension as it relates to Christ's love.

Comprehending the Incomprehensible

What is this love like? I don't know for sure, but I imagine that it is overwhelming. I imagine — based on our limited understanding of the fourth dimension — it is love that sees through us into the innermost being. It is radically intimate. It is love that pervades us, that permeates every aspect of our being, perhaps even down to the subatomic level. We cannot normally comprehend this. But when the Spirit of God is so filling us so that Jesus is dwelling in our hearts by faith, we are candidates for understanding this overwhelming, pervasive love.

Now I realize the word *pervasive* sounds unpleasant, but when used as an adjective to describe *love*, it sounds extremely pleasant, but pleasant in an overwhelming way. I have read in revival history of those who were so overwhelmed at times by the pervasive love of God, that they had to ask God to stop it, to stay His love, or they would die. While I cannot fathom death would be the end result, their testimony provides a glimpse into the overpowering nature of four-dimensional love. A modern writer — Ted Dekker in his novel *White* — attempts to illustrate this irrepressible love as a drowning sensation, having a magnificent climax in the very presence of Jesus.[34] However one describes it, four-dimensional love is something God wants us to experience as the ultimate expression of Christ's love for us.

The Fulness of God

Is four-dimensional love merely for the experience, for the feeling? Not at all! If it were, I might be nervous about it. According to Eph. 3:19, it is for one express purpose: *That ye might be filled with all the fulness of God.* To be filled with all the fulness of God, in this context, is to be immersed in the love of Christ to such an extent that His love overflows from your life to the lives of others. There is surely far more to this fulness than we could ever imagine. It may imply God taking possession of every aspect of our being, even down to the subatomic level, however that occurs. It is not for us to speculate too much. It is sufficient to know that His fulness, which follows on the heels of our grasping His four-dimensional love, is far greater than our eye has seen or our ear has heard or we have imagined. In this context, we read v. 20.

> Now unto him that is able to do exceeding abundantly above all that we ask or think, according to the power that worketh in us.
> Eph. 3:20

Exceeding abundantly means over and above, superabundantly, unmeasurably. It seems the tendency is to apply this verse in a superficial manner, by suggesting God can do things for us even beyond what we are expecting. While that is certainly true, it appears to be a very shallow understanding in this context of four-dimensional love. The phrase, *exceeding abundantly above all that we ask or think,* is very likely — in this context — a reference to God revealing four-dimensional love in our three-dimensional being. Words are inadequate to explain it. But it is a possibility because of *the power that worketh in us.* The capability is inside us, because the Holy Spirit, a multi-dimensional being, resides within our three-dimensional bodies.

With All Saints

There is one other condition for comprehending Christ's four-dimensional love. It is a simple modifying phrase found in v. 18 — *may be able to comprehend **with all saints**.* Notice the emphasis is not merely on the individual saint. The emphasis is on the corporate body of Christ — *all saints* (plural) — that, in a practical sense, finds its expression, at least as a starting point, at the level of a local church fellowship. Then v. 21 says, *Unto Him be glory in the church.* Of course, this reference to the church cannot be exclusively local church, because v. 21 goes on to say, *throughout all ages.* It is the entire body of Christ throughout church history. Here, I believe, is the point to be made: Christ is glorified, magnified, when His church experiences four-dimensional love.

I could be wrong about this, but it seems that we cannot fully experience four-dimensional love on this earth apart from other saints. God's working in our lives and His expression of love is not merely singular; it is plural. That is the nature of four-dimensional love. It doesn't see only single objects; it sees plural objects and the interconnectivity between them. The new age movement with its emphasis on "becoming one with everything," in my opinion, is largely wrong, but partly right. Isn't it just like Satan to take some truth and inject error? The error is seeking to become one with everything. The truth is saved people seeking to become one with Christ and with other believers in an organic union that only the Holy Spirit can produce. But notice that it's not an "every-man-for-himself" mentality. It is an understanding that we mutually grow together in Christ's love through unity.

So here's my understanding of the phrase, *with all saints*, in v. 18. The only way we can fully grasp Christ's four-dimensional love is in symphony with other Spirit-filled saints, and in a most immediate sense, that starts within the local church. You can, along with other believers in your local assembly, experience the four-dimensional love of God that overwhelms and fills with all the fulness of God in ways that we cannot begin to explain. When that happens, God is glorified, and Christ is magnified in His church.

I close the chapter with the words to a famous song entitled, *The Love of God*.[35]

> The love of God is greater far
> Than tongue or pen can ever tell;
> It goes beyond the highest star,
> And reaches to the lowest hell;
> Oh, love of God, how rich and pure!
> How measureless and strong!
> It shall forevermore endure—
> The saints' and angels' song.
>
> Could we with ink the ocean fill,
> And were the skies of parchment made,
> Were every stalk on earth a quill,
> And every man a scribe by trade;
> To write the love of God above
> Would drain the ocean dry;
> Nor could the scroll contain the whole,
> Though stretched from sky to sky.

---

[29] R.S. Beal Jr. and Earl D. Radmacher, *Ephesians* (Chino Valley, AZ: One World Press, 2012), p. 133.

[30] Warren W. Wiersbe, *The Bible Exposition Commentary: New Testament* (Colorado Springs, CO: Victor Books/Cook Communications, 2001), vol. 2, 31.

[31] Thomas L. Constable, *Notes on Ephesians* .pdf version http://www.soniclight.com/constable/notes/pdf/ephesians (accessed December, 2015), 51.

[32] Oswald J. Smith, "Deeper and Deeper" (No. 315) in *Great Hymns of the Faith*.

[33] "Tesseract," *Wikipedia: The Free Encyclopedia* (accessed Dec., 2015). (accessed Dec., 2015)

[34] Ted Dekker, *White* (Nashville, TN: Thomas Nelson Publ., 2009), metaphor used throughout the book.

[35] Frederick M. Lehman, "The Love of God" (No. 108) in *Rejoice Hymns*.

Chapter 10

Uniting to the Nth Degree

Virtually everyone desires peace on Earth and goodwill toward men. Although, we know that cannot happen fully until Jesus returns to launch His kingdom on Earth. Nevertheless, if the church of Jesus Christ were to become unified, the world would see a microcosm display of the peace and harmony Jesus will bring when He returns the second time. Unity in the body of Christ is a beautiful reflection to the world of unity in the Godhead.

Is unity within the church a far-fetched, utopian ideal, or is it an achievable goal? God's expectation for His church is unity. To that end, He has gifted certain men to lead the church to the point of unity.

> He gave some, apostles; and some, prophets; and some, evangelists; and some, pastors and teachers; for the perfecting of the saints, for the work of the ministry, for the edifying of the body of Christ: till we all come in the unity of the faith, and of the knowledge of the Son of God, unto a perfect man, unto the measure of the stature of the fulness of Christ. Eph. 4:11-13

The ultimate goal of church ministry is unity of the body unto perfection, unity that measures up to Christ's fulness. That is a tall order, but it is God's standard and, as we have discussed in previous chapters, He has given the provision through the Holy Spirit for accomplishing this level of unity. God considers it an attainable goal.

Unto him be glory in the church by Christ Jesus throughout all ages, Eph. 3:21. In the last chapter we learned that Christ is glorified — or we could say *magnified* — when we comprehend the four-dimensional aspect of Christ's love, to the end that we are filled with all the fulness of God. But it does not end there. There is one more level. God wants us to move from individual love to corporate love, from a few loving to many loving within His body. That results in unity. The church cannot glorify God apart from unity, and so Paul moves from this ascription of praise in Eph. 3 to a discussion of the means of unity in Eph. 4. In a nutshell, the means of unity is having the divine mindset, a concept we introduced in Chapter 1. It is now time to bring our thesis full-circle. In this final chapter we shall see the divine mindset in action in the church of Jesus Christ, and the end result is far more glorious than we could imagine.

Christ is magnified when you, along with other members of His body, love one another, becoming unified unto a perfect man, in conformity to Christ's fulness.

This is superlative unity — unity to the nth degree. Unfortunately, the church knows little of unity. Strife and contention and bitterness characterize many churches. People often leave churches because they can't get along with others, or they fight within the church, and churches split because of the infighting. God calls it earthly, sensual and demonic (James 3:15). The root problems are selfishness and pride, which are the opposite of *agape*-type love. The testimony of Christ is marred by a lack of love, but it is upheld by a spirit of genuine, Christlike love. Jesus said, *By this shall all men know that ye are my disciples, if ye have love one to another*, John 13:35. If Christ is glorified in the church when believers are unified, then we must seek to be unified at all costs. Of course, there must be rightness of doctrine, for that is one of the conditions of unity.

Unity is not inherently within you. Of yourself, you can never produce a spirit of sweet unity; your flesh is too selfish. But the same unity that characterizes the Godhead dwells within you, and His name is Holy Spirit. He can produce unity in your soul and He can produce unity between souls, but He'll never force you into it. You must choose to appropriate His provision. Let us now examine Eph. 4 and note three characteristics of unity.

> I therefore, the prisoner of the Lord, beseech you that ye walk worthy of the vocation wherewith ye are called, with all lowliness and meekness, with longsuffering, forbearing one another in love; endeavouring to keep the unity of the Spirit in the bond of peace. Eph. 4:1-3

Eph. 4 begins with the word *therefore*, which is a word of summary, conclusion and application. Paul is saying that, in light of what he has just written, certain actions need to take place

Unity Commences *Individually* by Walking Worthy

We are urged here in v. 1 to *walk worthy*, that is, appropriately, or in a manner that is fitting. To walk is to take reiterated steps, one step after another. You cannot take the next step until you have taken the last one. Of course, that implies it doesn't happen all at once, but over the process of time, as you learn to walk or live in an obedient manner, in a manner befitting your *vocation*, which is your calling.

What is our *calling*? It is that to which we have been called or invited. Some would say it is referring to our salvation, and certainly that is the starting point. However, that seems to be too broad of an answer. Our calling is much more specific than that.

> Who hath saved us, and called us with an holy calling, not according to our works, but according to his own purpose and grace, which was given us in Christ Jesus before the world began. 2 Tim. 1:9

Salvation itself is not our calling, but it is that which initiates our calling. The calling is distinct from the salvation. To what, then, have saints been called (i.e., invited)? Saints are called to holiness. God wants us to live holy lives, obedient unto Him. If you are not living in holiness, then you are not walking worthy of your calling.

Wherefore the rather, brethren, give diligence to make your calling and election sure: for if ye do these things, ye shall never fall. 2 Peter 1:10

Peter cannot be speaking of salvation from eternal condemnation, because there is nothing we can do to make that sure. Christ has done it all. To suggest here that our calling is our salvation is to imply that we must work for it by exercising diligence to make it sure. That is not how salvation is obtained. We are saved by grace through faith alone, not of works. Peter must be speaking of matters of sanctification. So our calling is not to salvation, per se. Our calling is to holiness of life. All are invited — indeed, commanded — to be holy, but not all accept the invitation. Recognizing this, Paul urges the saints to walk in a manner that is befitting our calling unto holiness (Eph. 4:1).

Lowly and Meek (v. 2). Jesus said, *Take my yoke upon you, and learn of me; for I am meek and lowly in heart,* Matt. 11:29. To be *lowly* is not to go around in life with a long face. To be meek is not to be wimpy and never stand for anything. To be lowly is to recognize your unworthiness apart from Christ. It is humbleness of mind. It is the idea of Phil. 2:5, *Let this mind be in you which was also in Christ Jesus.* It is the opposite of pridefulness. To be *meek* is to accept your circumstances as of the Lord even if they are difficult or dire. Most people react to unpleasant circumstances in bitterness, anger, or frustration. But meek people receive them with a Christlike spirit, knowing all things work together for good. So this calling, this holiness of life to which we are invited, is lowly and meek.

Longsuffering and Forbearing (v. 2). This is the idea of putting up with others, even if they are unkind or ungracious or mean-spirited. It is not responding in kind, but in Christlikeness. It is enduring under the pressure of prickly people, being tolerant of their quirky ways that might annoy you. People will surely get under your skin, so to speak, but if you are going to walk worthy of your calling unto holiness, then you must bear up with graciousness, by the grace of God.

Endeavoring to Keep the Unity of the Spirit (v. 3). Notice we don't ever have to try to create unity, for that is the Holy Spirit's job. He has already unified saints — we all have the same bond. We are called to *keep* the unity He has already provided. The word *keep* means to guard or protect. Selfishness and pride destroy the unity. When we are walking worthy, we are endeavoring — literally, making a diligent effort — to maintain the unity and peace of the Holy Spirit that is ours by inheritance. Of course, this means that choices must be made to submit to one another in joyfulness and to protect the unity that is ours in Christ. We must be diligent about it.

The Seven-Fold Basis for Unity

Paul, then, reminds of the seven-fold basis for unity. Seven is God's number of perfection.

> There is one body, and one Spirit, even as ye are called in one hope of your calling; One Lord, one faith, one baptism, One God and Father of all, who is above all, and through all, and in you all. Eph. 4:4-6

One Body. I am glad Paul did not say one church, because then some would claim universalism. Others would claim their local church to be the right church, implying all others are not right. Still others would rally around denominations as the basis for unity. No, the Bible says, *one body*. That is significant. What this means is that individuals from every kindred and tongue and people and nation become one in organic union with Christ. We become part of His body. Eph. 5:30 says, *For we are members of His body, of His flesh, and of His bones*. What a profound thought! For a body to function properly, there must be unity.

One Spirit. Within your spirit dwells the same Holy Spirit who dwells within my spirit. Our God is omnipresent and lives within everyone that is a child of God. What a unifying bond!

One Hope of Your Calling. Remember, your calling is unto holiness. The hope of your calling is the expectation that you can appropriate Christ's holiness and thereby be confident of reward at His Judgment Seat. Further, the hope of our calling is the attainment of glory and majesty that is to be intimately shared with Christ for all eternity in the Kingdom of God. We all have that prospect of reward, and we should strive for it together.

One Lord. Of course, this is referring to the Lord Jesus Christ. Perhaps a beautiful picture of the sevenfold basis for unity is the Jewish menorah. In Old Testament times, a huge menorah could be found in the tabernacle. It was made of gold and had seven lamps — three on the left and three on the right, with one prominent lamp in the center. The center lamp represents Christ, and I do not believe it to be merely coincidental that Paul places Jesus at the center of the seven-fold basis for unity, because the plan of God is fulfilled in His Son Jesus, who has been exalted. He is central in our understanding of unity. Indeed, He has made it possible by His death and resurrection and exaltation. It is only reasonable that He is the head of the one body.

One Faith. Notice there are not many faiths, but only one faith, one body of truth, as taught in the Scriptures. It includes not only salvation from eternal condemnation, but also sanctification, the saving of the soul unto reward. Believers will only experience unity with the brethren to the extent they are rallying around this central truth. Apart from this truth, there can be no true unity. Ironically, ecumenism — a movement whose aim is to unite all so-called Christian faiths — is Satan's deceptive means of perverting true unity.

One Baptism. This does not appear to be a reference to water baptism, but rather to the spiritual transaction that takes place at salvation, as described in Rom. 6:4-6. Some believe it refers to the Holy Spirit's immersion of believers into the body of Christ at the point of salvation, based on 1 Cor. 12:13. Others would say — based on the Greek wording of the same passage — it is Christ's immersion of believers in the Holy Spirit when they are saved. Either way, we know from other Scriptures passages that the Holy Spirit takes up residence in the lives of believers, and yet it is also true to say we are *in Christ*. The point to be made here is that all believers are united with Christ and the Holy Spirit because of the marvelous spiritual oneness we share with Him.

One God and Father of All. He is above all; He transcends. He is through all; His power pervades. He is in you all; He indwells you, and that makes this quite personal. The very clear point Paul is making is that believers already possess unity because God lives within. Our duty is to keep it — protect it; guard it; maintain it diligently.

Disunity in the Church of Jesus Christ

Is this kind of unity evident on a broad scale today in the church of Jesus Christ? No, for churches are full of prideful and selfish people who are combative and confrontational, and ready to fight — not the enemy, but one another. Because this sin problem is rife in Christian homes, it is also rampant in local churches. And because it is running wild in local churches, the body of Christ is not unified in the world. The world sees it and scorns, wanting nothing to do with the church. As a result, Christ is not being glorified in His church. Yet He so desires that His church magnify His holy name by holy living that leads to love and unity.

If believers in the future eternal realm will mirror the present church on Earth, then there will be multitudes of walls in Heaven, sectioning it into distinct and separate cities or zones. Believers will be segregated into schismatic groups, as is the case theoretically on Earth at the present time. Furthermore, there will need to be heavenly policemen patrolling the streets to keep conflict under control. Thankfully, it will not happen that way. Our blurred vision will be made clear.

Earnestly Contending or Earnestly Contentious?

A tragedy within a segment of modern fundamentalist Christianity — which wears *earnestly contend for the faith* (Jude 3) as a sort of badge of honor — is that unity is disrupted as brethren "earnestly contend" with one another over nonessentials, making virtually every issue a doctrine over which to separate. Many are proclaiming, *Thus saith the Lord God, when the Lord hath not spoken*, Ezek. 22:28, pressing their particular standards on others. Now I fully understand the importance of the command to *earnestly contend*. It is intended to keep us from apostasy and ecumenism. Yes, the basis for unity is truth. But using *earnestly contend* as an excuse for being "earnestly contentious," combative, and mean-spirited toward those with whom you disagree is twisting the Scriptures and robbing the church of unity.

The bond of unity is love. Where's the love in Christianity, particularly amongst those who hold to core truth? I firmly believe those who diligently maintain unity here and now on Earth will be the ones who will rule with Jesus then. Those who disrupt unity now will be in the darkness outside of His ruling realm. There is much at stake!

Unity Develops *Corporately* Through Perfecting

After emphasizing our individual responsibility as believers to walk worthy and thereby promote unity, Paul changes gears and talks about corporate unity within the body.

> But unto every one of us is given grace according to the measure of the gift of Christ. Eph. 4:7

He starts the discussion about corporate unity by highlighting grace as the catalyst for unity. Every believer has been given grace — the divine enablement to do what God wants you to do. In this case, the grace is in the form of gifting. Verse eight refers to Christ giving spiritual *gifts unto men*. The gifts are various, according to the measure of the gift of Christ. A more exhaustive list of spiritual gifts can be found in Rom. 12 and 1 Cor. 12. Don't expect your gift or gifts to be the same as others. Gifts vary from individual to individual. It is not for us to question. God is the One to determine who receives what gifts — and all gifts are to be used for His glory.

After a parenthesis in vs. 8-10, Paul hones in on the gifts of leadership that impact the corporate body in a public fashion.

> He gave some, apostles; and some, prophets; and some, evangelists; and some, pastors and teachers. Eph. 4:11

These are gifts that God bestows upon certain individuals for helping the corporate body to develop in unity. To that end, some were given the gifts of apostleship and prophecy. These gifts, I believe, were relegated to the early church. Eph. 2:20 indicates the church was *built upon the foundation of the apostles and prophets*. The foundation was laid long ago, in the first century. Thus, these gifts are no longer being given by God today, their purpose having been already accomplished.

Next we read of gifts that are valid for our age and for the ultimate purpose of developing corporate unity — evangelists, pastors and teachers — or pastor-teachers. Evangelists may be referring to itinerant preachers of the gospel, such as Philip the evangelist in the early church. But they could also include one or more within the church who are gifted, passionate proclaimers of the gospel and, as such, serve as stimulants in the church for promoting evangelism. Of course, we are all called to evangelize in some way, but I have no doubt that some are gifted with a unique ability to articulate gospel truth clearly. It could be the evangelists are also capable of proclaiming the gospel to the saints, which is a gospel of sanctification. Of course, the pastor-teacher is the shepherd who leads the local church and patiently ministers to the congregation by shepherding and teaching the Word. The gifts themselves are not as critical to our discussion, as is the *purpose* for the gifts. Notice the contribution of these gifted leaders to the local church, if they are using their God-given gifts properly.

> For the perfecting of the saints, for the work of the ministry, for the edifying of the body of Christ. Eph. 4:12

In the original language, vs. 11-12 read as one long sentence. God gifts certain men to lead corporately in perfecting the saints to do the work of the ministry so the body of Christ is edified. Some church folks think the work of the ministry is solely the job of the pastor. They envision a football-team model, with the deacons as players and the pastor as quarterback. The church members view the game from the stands. That is incorrect thinking. Actually, the ministry is the duty of all saints, including the pastor. A more appropriate illustration would be the church out on the playing field, with the pastor serving as the coach — encouraging, shepherding, teaching, and coaching the players. The world watches from the stands.

If these gifted leaders are serving according to their God-given gifts, then what will be the result? The church body will be *perfected*. The word means equipped. The church body will be completely furnished to do the work of the ministry and the body will be edified, or built up. What if those gifted as evangelists and pastor-teachers are not using their gifts for this intended purpose in the church? The body of Christ will not be equipped to do the work of the ministry, and the church will not be edified. That would be a tragedy indeed, because unity develops corporately through perfecting. When the servant of the Lord is not using His God-given gifts, or when the congregation is resisting His leadership, the ultimate goal will not be reached. On the other hand, when both parties are functioning according to God's plan, the end result is most beautiful.

Unity Culminates *Ultimately* in Plural Becoming Singular

> Till we all come in the unity of the faith, and of the knowledge of the Son of God, unto a perfect man, unto the measure of the stature of the fulness of Christ: Eph. 4:13

Notice the phrase, *a perfect man*. When saints, individually, are walking worthily, and when they are being developed corporately by men that God gifts specifically for this purpose, then the church body — comprised of many individuals — will become one perfect man. Plural will become singular. *Many* will become *one*, that is, one in heart and one in soul like the early church; not ceasing to be individuals, but becoming individuals in symphony with others. Imagine a hundred musicians who have individually matured in the performance of their respective instruments, coming together under the leadership of a gifted conductor and performing in perfect harmony, producing the sweetest sounds imaginable. That is in essence what God is describing in this verse. Unity amongst saints that crescendos in the beauty of Christlikeness. Incidentally, the word *perfect* in this verse does not mean sinless. Sinlessness is impossible in this life. The word *perfect* means complete, mature, having arrived at the goal. It is the same basic word used by Jesus on the cross, when He cried, *It is finished*, John 19:30.

This is the ultimate, when saints jointly enter into glorious heaven-on-earth living, and it only happens when many become one, when they come *unto the measure of the stature of the fulness of Christ.* We also saw the phrase *fulness of God* in Chapter 9, when explaining Eph. 3:19. Paul's prayer is that we *might be filled with all the fulness of God.* In this context, we are filled with all His fulness by experiencing Christ's four-dimensional love. How do we experience that depth of love? According to Eph. 3:18, we experience it *with all saints.* What this means is that love of this nature is experienced only when the saints are walking together in unity, unto the measure of the stature of the fulness of Christ.

> From whom the whole body fitly joined together and compacted by that which every joint supplieth, according to the effectual working in the measure of every part, maketh increase of the body unto the edifying of itself in love. Eph. 4:16

The bond of unity is love. I long to reach that goal; don't you? Incidentally, Paul does not expect this will happen only after life has ended and we are in the presence of Christ. No, he expects it to happen now! But is this level of Christian maturity and love and unity evident predominantly in the church of Jesus Christ in our age? Tragically, it is not. Perhaps there are four possible reasons why even local assemblies have not yet reached this goal:

1. The individuals within the church have not been walking worthy of their calling.
2. The gifted leaders of the church have neglected their God-given responsibility to develop the church unto unity, perhaps because their own life is not right or maybe because their focus is on the wrong things in ministry.
3. The church members are carnal and refuse to be led.
4. All of the above.

God forgive us for selfishness and pride that stand in the way of His desire to bring us *unto a perfect man, unto the measure of the stature of the fulness of Christ.* Oh, may we magnify the Lord Jesus Christ by our lives, bringing glory to His name!

Scripture Index

Made in the USA
Monee, IL
09 January 2021